Biblical Principles to Prosperity

How You Can Become Prosperous by Following
God's Word

Israel C. Wright, MSA, CFE, AAMS

Biblical Principles to Prosperity

Many of us seek more; more fulfillment, more purpose, more happiness or more wealth. In short, we seek prosperity. But it seems the more we seek it, the more it eludes us! Could it be that we are looking for prosperity in the wrong places? Could we be going about the search incorrectly? Is our idea of prosperity faulty? What would you do if you had the opportunity to learn the path, procedures and techniques to acquiring the 'more' that you seek? Would you grab the opportunity? Would you open the door? And more importantly, once you learned the procedures, would you apply them?

The plagues that are running rampant –

"For the love of money is the root of all evil: which while some coveted after, they have erred from the faith, and pierced themselves through with many sorrows."
1 Tim 6:10

And

"For since the beginning of the world men have not heard, nor perceived by the ear, neither hath the eye seen, O God, beside thee, what he hath prepared for him that waiteth for him." *Isaiah 64:4*

The cures –

"But seek ye first the kingdom of God, and His righteousness; and all these things shall be added unto you." Matthew 6:33

and

"...Take heed that no man deceive you." Matthew 24:4

Let's begin your path to prosperity…

Best of all,

Israel C. Wright, MSA, CFE, AAMS

ISBN: 198192602X

ISBN: 9781981926022

This book is printed on acid-free paper.

1stBooks – rev. 08/20/03
CS – rev. 12/22/17

Acknowledgements

The first edition of this book was published in December 2003. It took over two and a half years to research and review different forms of scripture (Torah, King James, New International, Quran, Hebrew and Aramaic translations) to ensure the proper definitions and context of the verses. In the past 15 years, I have learned much more, spoken, counseled, consulted, and coached many more people, and began studying for a PhD in psychology.

In addition, since the first edition, I have travelled to and lived in other places. All of this has led me to believe that the insight I originally received was valid and applicable to our (yours, mine, and others) daily lives. For this, I thank my God, Jehovah Jireh, as He is the provider of all that I am and have. He has blessed me with the insight and ability to comprehend and retain a great majority of the philosophical, humanistic, and financial information I have encountered. He has blessed me with the experiences and situations (both good and bad) that have made me into who I am. Most importantly, He has blessed me with the ability to relay this information to others in a way that is most captivating and understood.

I thank my family who know and understand me and are always my sounding board and provide me with valuable input and perspective. Beyond measure, I thank and apologize to my wife who had to endure my personal and spiritual challenges and struggles. And finally, I thank my clients, each of whose support taught me many invaluable lessons and confirmed for me exactly what I am supposed to be doing.

Best of all,

Professor Israel C. Wright, MSA, CFE, AAMS

Table of Contents

The Reward is Promised

I would like to first say that I am not any different from you. I have encountered in some form or another the same difficulties that you may have. I fight the same battles that you do - pride, greed, selfishness, confusion, and doubt. However, my uniqueness (if any) lies in the ammunition I use in waging these wars. I live with the edict issued by Jesus firmly planted within me:

"Take heed that no man deceive you." Matthew 24:4

From that directive, I aligned the words of Solomon:

"Wisdom is the principle thing; therefore get wisdom; and with all thy getting, get understanding." Proverbs 4:7

Thus, I am always seeking to learn the answers to the questions that an investigator asks – who, what, when, where, how and (most importantly) why. I then use the painstakingly researched information to guide my actions to achieve the most benefit for myself and for others. It is by this method of 'seeking and finding' that I have been blessed to learn what I've learned, gotten to where I am and author this book.

Although I am a licensed stockbroker, insurance agent and real estate salesperson and can give you appropriate financial information, this book is neither designed nor intended to give you detailed financial advice. And as a financial advisor, I have witnessed the results of many people who apply the techniques of financial self-help books. I have seen how some of these people have been left feeling empty. Some, even though they have achieved their financial objective, are still unfulfilled and unaware of their purpose in life. They themselves may even tell you that they are happy and content. And if they aren't downright lying, they may be misinformed as to what true happiness is. I am sure we can agree that happiness lies neither in material possessions, power nor status.

On the other hand, I have also witnessed others who are truly happy with their finances, their lives, and themselves. These people are content with their possessions, thankful for their health, appreciative of their friends and family and want for nothing. I am not comparing these two types of people to say that sound financial practices are ineffective or damaging but instead to illustrate that one's foundation does not have to rest on finances for true prosperity to be recognized and realized.

Furthermore, this book is not intended to debunk or replace the teachings of pastors, preachers, or other clergy. Although I am an ordained minister, I do not profess to know everything about the Bible and its scriptures. I am being obedient and sharing with you the lessons, insight and information I have personally received in my life.

This book's intent is to show you the basic principles that lead to prosperity. You may wonder how and why the seven actions contained in this book have been selected as foundational. As you will see, these principles are the cornerstone of all that we do – mentally, emotionally, physically and financially. These principles are all encompassing and comprise each of the bottom line issues we deal with in our lives. Of course, sometimes one principle is more heavily weighted in different situations, but I daresay that *never* do any of us encounter something in our lives that does not contain these principles.

Within this book, I hope you can (and will) identify your own issues, problems and habits. This will provide you the opportunity to receive validation of the principles you are already activating or to see what you may need to improve on. Either way, this book's objective is to empower you with the basic truths of the universe so you can utilize them. I pray that arming you with this critically necessary (and oftentimes deliberately omitted) information will enable you to make a difference in your life and in the lives of those whom you hold dear. One of the key benefits of this information is that you can use it in the way you see fit to assist you in accomplishing your earthly purpose.

Since some of you reading this book may not believe as I do, and possibly have not been exposed to the financial principles as I have, I humbly request that you be open-minded and genuinely and unashamedly focus on your relationship with God, yourself and your fellow man. I ask that you review, contemplate and reflect on your own beliefs, feelings and habits. Also, identify the origin of all the information that made you who you are, as this is vitally important. The identification of the source of your information is critical in determining its validity, reliability, and credibility. It is written:

"Beloved, believe not every spirit, but try the spirits whether they are of God: because many false prophets are gone out into the world." 1 John 4:1

After doing this, I truly believe that you will be receptive to the ideas and information contained in this book. I pray that you become aware of the causes of your personal (and financial) troubles as well as learn the solutions to fix them.

Lest I be misunderstood, I would like to clarify something. I am not guaranteeing success or financial prosperity even if you believe and activate all the principles. Indeed, we operate under the simultaneous laws of cooperation (Genesis 1:28-30) and resistance (Genesis 3:17-19). I will say that if you genuinely believe, adopt, and practice these principles, you will receive a new peace and fulfillment that far exceeds any monetary wealth! If I were to guarantee prosperity in a monetary sense I would be saying that I know the will of God for each of you. I don't.

Generally, we do not know why God does what he does. We do know however, that *"His will be done"* and *"all things work together for good."* Hence, if I were to activate the principles and never receive prosperity, or my idea of success, then it just might be that my idea of prosperity or success is not what God knows to be best and wants for me. I can rest in knowing that my 'failure' is somehow glorifying God. I can have faith that someone somewhere has reached God through witnessing (or hearing of) my trials.

"And his disciples asked him, saying, Master, who did sin, this man, or his parents, that he was born blind? Jesus answered, neither hath this man sinned, nor his parents; but that the works of God should be made manifest in him." John 9:2-3

This 'failure' can create quite a stir and be an area of controversy. In my own family, I have heard some disparage another's act of faith. The one who is doubtful or unaware of the principles criticizes the one who believes and practices the principles. This occurs because the criticizer does not see the believer's reward the same way as the believer does. This difference of perception may be attributed to a different definition of prosperity between the believer and the criticizer. The thing to be thankful for (and to pray for) is that the person acting on faith does not lose his faith or view the outcome as a failure.

When the believer begins to lose his faith because he does not see his reward, it is a dangerous situation! Before we get to that point and to prevent this from occurring, we can rejoice in a few things - -

One, God is not limited by time; only we mortals are on a time clock! While He may plan to reward us for our faith, it may come at a time different than we would prefer. (You will read that patience is one of the principles.)

Second, our perception of success and prosperity may be a little faulty. We might just be a little selfish! We may have to endure some trials and learn some lessons before we recognize and align ourselves with God's will. And after we agree, we may see that we didn't want 'that ol' thing' anyway.

Or lastly, it may not be good for us overall. We have all heard the saying 'be careful what you wish for.' God, exercising His Fatherly wisdom, may withhold what we ask for because He knows that what we want (and are praying for) isn't good for us. (If you have children or nieces and nephews, I am sure you can relate.)

But to keep you from becoming discouraged or feel you are reading this book for no reason, let me remind you that God is a god of His word and is not a 'respecter of persons.' This means that if you practice the principles, God will honor it. However, be reminded that the reward may come in a different form and at a different time than you expected or wanted.

Have you ever had something truly wonderful happen through a negative experience? For example, you may be working to get a new car, but instead your current car gets wrecked in a fender bender. But what you don't know is that the accident is the catalyst to put you in the situation to receive a new car from a source you had no idea about! Alas, having your car wrecked is really a blessing in disguise.

Before the accident you wondered how you were going to trade in the old clunker and how you were going to come up with the money for the down payment, and with your credit history, who was going to give you the loan for the car. But now, your worries seem to have just multiplied! Oh, sure, on top of everything before, you now wonder how you will be able to trade in the *wrecked* clunker. The answer is simpler than we make it; leave it to God and He will provide. After all, Jesus told us:

"Therefore I tell you, do not worry about your life, what you will eat or drink; or about your body, what you will wear. Is not life more important than food, and the body more important than clothes? Look at the birds of the air; they do not sow or reap or store away in barns, and yet your heavenly Father feeds them. Are you not much more valuable than they? Who of you by worrying can add a single hour to his life?"
Matthew 6:25-27 (NIV)

This life becomes easier to deal in (and with) once we learn to be happy with what we have. By learning and activating the principles, you will acquire the peace that comes with identifying and walking the path to prosperity. More importantly, remember that the ultimate reward is not here on this earth.

"Rejoice and be exceedingly glad: for great is your reward in heaven: for so persecuted they the prophets which were before you."
Matthew 5:12

Here is the dealmaker - - activating these principles opens the door to a more prosperous and peaceful life and puts your name in the "Book of Life."

Be, Know, Do...More

Introduction

Each of us today suffers from many different stresses. These stressors are too numerous to list and their causes varied. In the psychological field, issues are attributed to either nature (your genetic and biological make up) and nurture (your upbringing, home life, relationships, and environment.) As varied as the influences may be in the physical world, these stresses share one common (and spiritual) origin – sin. These stresses come into being from our failure to obey the life-enhancing principals illustrated, stated and practiced in the Bible. These principles, which have been set out for our benefit, are unwavering, unchanging constants that must oblige their activation (or inactivation.)

The Bible clearly promises a reward to anyone who, through obedience, practices the principles contained within it.

"This book of the law shall not depart out of thy mouth, but thou shalt meditate therein day and night, that thou mayest observe to do according to all that is written therein; for then thou shalt make thy way prosperous, and then thou shalt have good success." Joshua 1:8

As this book refers to quotations, the reader may not see the written (or expected) benefit from applying the principals. To clarify this potential area of confusion, please refer to Joshua 1:8. *"Then thou shalt have good success,"* is the promise to all who apply the principals written in the law. Remember; success is synonymous with prosperity.

So, while many of the verses have results (either promises or punishments) within them, many do not. But the reader can at any time refer to Joshua 1:8 to see the implied promise in any verse where one is not explicit or clearly defined.

As mentioned earlier, the source of your information and education is vitally important. Your experiences, exposure and education are major factors in creating your beliefs, values and actions. Personally, I learned through my experiences that in general, the world doesn't want anyone to succeed (prosper). To provide a little insight on the credibility of the sources, consider this. Jesus said that Satan has an objective:

"The thief cometh not, but for to steal, and to kill, and to destroy:"
John 10:10

Jesus also refers to Satan as the *"prince of this world" (John 12:31.)* Jesus tells us that Satan is the ruler of this realm! Therefore, we can ascertain from the authorities of a prince, from the nature of Satan and from the words of Jesus that any information or guidance we get from a worldly source (any source that is not from the word of God) will eventually destroy us. This is what makes Matthew 24:4 so vitally important!

To test this principle, let's use something we are all familiar with – food. In the beginning, God created and set out those things that were beneficial for our bodies. And considering that our bodies were originally intended to last forever, we can assume that the original diet was designed to keep our bodies at optimum health and efficiency.

"And God said, Behold, I have given you every herb bearing seed, which is upon the face of all the earth, and every tree, in the which is the fruit of a tree yielding seed; to you it shall be for meat." Genesis 1:29

This diet was shown to be effective by Belteshazzar, Shadrach, Meshach, and Abednego. *(Daniel 1)*

Fast forward to today......

Today, a meal deal from any fast food location is less expensive than the average pound of cherries. In addition, fast food is generally more convenient and less time consuming than preparing a home cooked meal. But for some strange reason, cherries are more filling and physiologically satisfying than a double hamburger! What is wrong with this picture?

With the advent of two income homes, single parent households, increased taxes, the media (and advertisements), and other "worldly" creations, we have drifted away from a healthier diet. And with the principles being true, we have experienced the consequences of this drifting. It is easy to site the increased obesity among our population and all the social, mental and physical problems associated with obesity. If we consider the recent lawsuits against fast food restaurants, we can now add monetary effects.

I believe that the prince of this world has *craftily* designed this predicament. But we can arm and protect ourselves. We as believers, are told to

"...be not conformed to this world: but be ye transformed by the renewing of your mind, that ye may prove what is that good, and acceptable, and perfect will of God." Romans 12:2

This renewing of our minds includes the learning and embracing of the Biblical principles. We must toss out the unprofitable "worldly" teachings, idioms and practices and activate the biblical principles. It is only when we do this that we become obedient and fulfill the will of God.

There was a time

"...when we were children, we were in slavery under the basic principles of the world." Galatians 4:3 (NIV)

But my friend, we are free. We are no longer enslaved because as awakened spiritual beings, we made a choice to renew our minds and make ourselves different from the rest of the world. But, let's not forget that, in addition to being told to renew our minds, we are told

"See to it that no one takes you captive through hollow and deceptive philosophy, which depends on human tradition and the basic principles of this world rather than on Christ." Colossians 2:8 (NIV)

It is evident and very clear that the Bible tells us to separate ourselves from this world. How do we separate ourselves? By focusing on Christ. And the only way we can focus on Christ is by building, nurturing and increasing a relationship with Him. It is only through this relationship that we will find our purpose.

What are the key components to building a successful relationship? The general answer is trust. But how what must be done to build trust? To build a relationship, there must be frequency and proximity. In other words, how often are you in communication and how physically close you are to the other person. Think of the relationship you built with your best friend; you generally spent a lot of time talking and being with that person. My siblings are the closest people to me and after that are my Army buddies - all the time and experiences we've shared has built a solid relationship. But also think of the flip side – long distance relationships are generally known to not work very well. The trust is hard to build if there isn't frequent communication and the distance between the two forms is great.

These concepts bring to question two of the world's adages –

"absence makes the heart grow fonder"

and

"out of sight, out of mind."

In the two adages we can see two completely opposite outcomes for the same situation. The only way that I can explain the difference between them is that they are a reflection of the flesh and the hypocrisy of it and the world. Overall, regardless of which concept is used, the importance of frequency and proximity in building and maintaining relationships remains.

Jesus maintained His relationship through the frequency and proximity displayed through His frequent prayer. From that prayer came the recognition of His purpose. Indeed, His purpose was so great, that he asked for it to be removed (Matthew 26:39, 42). However, the trust built in the relationship empowered Him to believe in the purpose of His calling and to have the courage and discipline to see it through. I daresay that with the knowledge and acceptance of one's purpose comes fulfillment, and with the fulfillment comes inner peace. And I am sure you can agree that inner peace is the remedy for greed, fear, selfishness and low self-esteem and thus is the vaccine for all evil.

I believe that this inner peace is what every human being searches for his or her entire life. The void that exists in an individual without this peace is often filled with drugs, alcohol, gratuitous sex, hostility, apathy, and depression. In the field of psychology the void is viewed as an internal conflict termed cognitive dissonance. The general responses to cognitive dissonance are maladaptive behaviors (as mentioned, alcohol abuse, overeating, drug use, promiscuity, and the like). These damaging and harmful use of substances or behaviors are an attempt to achieve release, relief, or escape (from the situation causing the internal conflict.) In other words, they are attempts to fill the void that can only be filled through a relationship with the Most High.

This self-destruction can be seen and assessed by anyone who is grounded in the foundation of the principles. The question left unanswered is, "If it can be seen, why doesn't everyone recognize it?" Remember the craftily designed world that seeks to destroy us? Let's identify what is necessary to learn and become grounded in the principles and find out why so many fail to do so.

Generally, personal growth is a culmination of a person's experiences, relationships and knowledge. These three things however are of no significance and will not produce personal growth if the individual does not muse (internalize and reflect) on how they come to be, what they do, what they mean and how they affect the individual. This "musing" is usually done in two environments – when the person is in a positive social circle (usually family and friends) and when the person is alone.

The musing that occurs when a person is with his family tends to focus on his origin, his purpose, his effect on others and his sense of belonging. This reflection incites growth in interpersonal relationships (unity and community), responsibilities, obligations and consequences.

When the person is alone (especially in a natural environment), he may muse on his gratitude, his future, his goals, his history, his relationships and himself as a person. These areas provoke invaluable growth in all aspects of his life and are necessary to attain the awareness that is conducive for success (prosperity.)

If we were to go back 100-150 years, we would see that people had two main sources of 'amusement' - social and individual events. Yes, we have those today also, but there is a radical difference. In years past, the social events were with family and exhibited some type of hierarchy, respect, reverence and loyalty. Going back to what occurs when an individual is in a positive social environment, this setting was (is) optimum.

When a person was alone, his activities were generally work, reading, writing or overall creating something. These activities were (and still are) the best conductors of meditation and self-reflection.

In today's world, amusement often comes from shallow, fickle and frivolous activities that lead to immediate gratification but provide little, if any, long-term growth. Generally, this amusement possesses no development value and creates intolerance for activities that are tedious or have a delayed reward. These activities create individuals who want to always be entertained or amused (TV, video games, food). As a result, because they are focusing on external sources of amusement, people may become afraid of being alone or looking within themselves. They may also develop the attitude of "the easy way" or "quick money" in most things that they do. To witness examples of this, listen to today's 'music" that is moving yet deceptive, void, and manipulative.

This situation exists because the world has created tools, vehicles and systems that preoccupy individuals and keep them from doing those things necessary to achieve growth and develop a relationship with Christ. The system's creation of additional burdens to preoccupy our daily lives is not new; Pharaoh did the same thing to keep the Israelites from receiving Moses.

"Let there more work be laid upon the men, that they may labour therein; and let them not regard vain words." Exodus 5:9

When a person is worried about how he is going to pay his electric bill or how he is going to finance a new(er) car, what is the likelihood he is going to reflect on his blessings and thank God? What are the chances that he is going to think about his neighbor's welfare? What are the chances he will think of himself outside of his physical and worldly needs?

In psychology, Dr. Abraham Maslow created the Hierarchy of Human Needs. The first and base level are physical -food, water, clothing, warmth, shelter. Dr. Maslow terms the levels 'preponent' which means that if one does not have the level fulfilled, the next level has little chance of receiving thought or focus. Indeed, I have been cold with no relief in sight. And there was no other thought entering my mind other than achieving warmth and escaping the situation. No thoughts of my wife, my kids, my bills, or my favorite anything! Just the focus of warmth!

The world is so effective at creating situations of lack, that this lack becomes a preoccupation for even those of us who have a relationship with the Most High. This causes us to forget that we are to operate on another level. We are lead astray by the doubt, ignorance, fear, and greed the world instills in us.

"Since you died with Christ to the basic principles of this world, why, as though you still belonged to it, do you submit to its rules: Do not handle! Do not taste! Do not touch!" Colossians 2:20 (NIV)

We must remember that we should not *"love the world, neither the things that are in the world"* because *"if any man love the world, the love of the Father is not in him."* Fear, doubt, ignorance and greed are worldly creations fathered by sin. Separating ourselves from these things aligns us with love (God is love) and the rewards and promises that it offers.

I pray that by reading this book, you are beginning your journey towards true prosperity. I do believe and wholly submit that if you subscribe to and apply the *Biblical Principles to Prosperity*, you will become more prosperous in every area of your life.

"For all the promises of God are in him are yea, and in him Amen, unto the glory of God by us." 2 Corinthians 1:20

What is Prosperity?

As a financial advisor, I have encountered many different people who are in unique financial situations. However, in these situations, the similarities outnumber the differences. All of these people seek health, peace, success and happiness. All of them want to protect their family (physically and financially), retire while they are still young and healthy, and have enough money to do the things they enjoys. Race, gender, education, socio-economic status and religion are trivial categories that do not significantly influence a large variation in these people's overall objectives. What these categories do influence, however, is the *definition* of these objectives and the route taken to achieve them. I have found that the key characteristics that create an individual's financial status are the possessed knowledge and activation of the principles or conversely, the ignorance and failure to activate the principles. Thus, most negative situations are generally rooted in a failure to apply the principles while the positive situations are generally a result of successfully applying the principles.

Let's first clarify that prosperity is relative; it means different things to different people. It can mean good health, a unified family, an operating and reliable vehicle or having no debt. It has been taught and sometimes interpreted that God wants you to be financially rich because the Apostle John wrote

"Beloved, I wish above all things that thou mayest prosper and be in health, even as thy soul prospereth." 3 John 1:2

In my research I found that the original word that was interpreted as 'prosper' is euhodos ('eu'- well or good and 'hodos'- way or journey.) The Latin-based prefix 'eu' is translated as 'good.' You know words that use the prefix 'eu': euphemism (saying not so good things in a good way), Eugene (a man with good genetics,) and euthanize (putting someone or an animal down in a painless, good way.) From this, the word euhodos simply means is to get to where you are attempting to go or get done what you are trying to do. It has no particular attachment to material wealth. Personally, I believe that John was inspired by God and was writing with a pure perspective of prosperity and was not trying to mislead anyone. I find it rather significant that the words he used were not referencing money or any monetary element.

God Himself spoke the word 'prosper' in the book of Isaiah and neither time did it mean material wealth. *(Isaiah 54:17, 55:11.)* Again, all it means is to complete the intended task.

So, to infer that John said that God wants us to be materially wealthy or that you *'deserve'* to be wealthy is rather bold and misleading. And sad to say, this misleading has hurt quite a few people and has turned many from the church.

Even though prosperity can mean different things, its different interpretations share a common foundation. This foundation can be defined as satisfaction, achievement, or completion. As mentioned before, some may classify prosperity as having a million dollars, while others may classify prosperity as having their child return home. These differences, though individually based, have the same beginning premise of what brings that person peace of mind. And peace of mind is not just some short-term happiness, but a long-term fulfillment that comes from realization of a purpose that is in accordance with God's will. And this my dear reader, is the definition of prosperity that is used throughout this book.

Similarly, the Bible's principles are uniform. Each of the principles are rooted on the two charges that Jesus clarified to us:

"...Thou shalt love the Lord thy God with all thy heart, and with all thy soul, and with all thy mind. This is the first and great commandment. Matthew 22:37-38

And

"...Take heed that no man deceive you." Matthew 24:4

These two commandments are indeed the substance and foundation to every lesson, every scripture and every person in the Bible. As you increase your understanding and insight, you will see how each of the Biblical principles relates to these two commandments. Any additional explanation or clarification will not be necessary when your spiritual light bulb flashes on! And that, my friend, is a beautiful thing! And that is the whole purpose of this book.

However, please be aware that these basic principles are correlated. This correlation commands that the application of one mandates the application of the others for each of them to truly be effective.

Remember, individually they are *basic* principles but together they become complex.

Problems, issues and situations that we face daily incorporate contradictions to each of the principles. Therefore, you sometimes hear, "it isn't that easy" or "you don't understand; there is more to it than that." Ahhh…is that so? We have been taught that life isn't all black and white. It isn't? Here is why I believe that there is no easy or hard and that life *IS* black and white –Please follow me on this idea....

If you try to lift your refrigerator, you may find it hard to do. But if you lift a plate, you may find it easy to do. However, both assessments are incorrect if the item is assessed unto itself. The refrigerator is what it is and is designed to fulfill its purpose just as the plate is what it is and designed to fulfill its purpose. It is only when comparisons are made that we can make judgements of hard and easy, hard and soft, long and short, high and low. Comparing the two opens the door for frustration, resentment, and disappointment. Without the comparison, the item is just what it is and requires the energy (and work) that it does to utilize or achieve it.

This comparison is what keeps people from stepping up and doing those things that are required (this will be discussed in one of the principles.) This is also the beginning of that "gray area" in life.

Think of the Most High. He refers to Himself as "I am" (Exodus 3:14.) All good. Pure love. Can do no evil and is incapable of even thinking evil thoughts. Satan (translated as "the Great Deceiver") on the other hand is the exact opposite. All evil. Pure hatred. Can do no good and is incapable of thinking anything good. My friend, where is the gray area? *You* are the gray area!

The gray area is a mental position man creates to give him the freedom to not obey, stick to or activate the principles. The gray area is where we stand when we straddle the fence. And we know that *"a double minded man is unstable in all his ways" (James 1:8)* right? Due to our sinful nature, we want the pleasures of the flesh without the obligations of obeying the law. Unfortunately, we cannot *have our cake and eat it too.* God in His wisdom gave us choice, and it is up to us to decide with whom we will align ourselves. It is written,

"He that is not with me is against me; and he that gathereth not with me scattereth abroad." Matthew 12:30

With these words, Jesus tells us that there our choice is an absolute - either righteousness or sin. We can also clearly read what the consequences are for not gathering with Jesus. And don't we see them all the time? There are millions of people who are lost, drifting, searching for answers and purpose. In contrast, Jesus does not clearly define what the reward is for being with him. I believe we can safely infer here that the reward for gathering with Jesus is *'good success.'*

Jesus also tells us,

"No man can serve two masters: for either he will hate the one, and love the other; or else he will hold to the one, and despise the other." Matthew 6:24

Remember how cartoons portrayed the conscience? Remember the angel on one shoulder and an imp on the other? Don't we all have an internal battle akin to that? (Remember that cognitive dissonance that I mentioned?) An interesting question would be 'what are the internal components that are engaging in the conflict?' I believe the two components are our authentic essence (spirit) and our mind (earthly perceiver and translator). What is the deciding factor of which side we choose? We know that following the law takes discipline, strength, and is challenging in regard to the propensities and desires of the body. Those are the factors that leads following the law to be a less popular path. But simply put, the reward for choosing the Lord's path is immeasurable. But it is still a choice that must be made. Joshua knew this when he told the Israelites,

*"And if it seem evil unto you to serve the LORD, **choose** you **this day** whom ye will serve; whether the gods which your fathers served that were on the other side of the flood, or the gods of the Amorites, in whose land ye dwell: but as for me and my house, we will serve the LORD."* Joshua 24:15

With this, we can see that choice is an absolute, and there is no 'riding the fence.' Thus, we are living a lie if we choose to live in the gray area.

"He that saith, I know him, and keepeth not his commandments, is a liar, and the truth is not in him." 1 John 2:4

And since God knows all, this lie is one we are telling only to ourselves and does not alleviate us from the responsibility of doing the right thing. In layman's terms, this lie (gray area) is called an excuse! "I couldn't do it because…." "It didn't work because…" "See, what had happened was…." We have all heard them and done it ourselves. An excuse is just that; an excuse!

Contrary to popular belief, you do fail if all you do is try and failure *IS* an option! *("There is no such thing as failure as long as you try." and "Failure is not an option.")* If God ordained that I write this book, get it published and distributed but all I did was try to do so, then you wouldn't be reading it and I would have failed. Hmmm…it is the fact that I (all glory to God) DID obey and write this book, publish it and distribute it that fulfills His will. And for the sake of my brother, who demands all the details, let me clarify. If the book had been written, published, but not distributed, the objective would have not been met, so it too would have been a failure.

We must not be afraid to fail. We must be willing to go against the grain of society, our families, and our friends in the name and for the sake of the principles. We must be willing to work endlessly and sacrifice our all for His purpose. We must be willing to take the risks necessary to reach our objective. We must work to realize our purpose and fulfill it as God ordained it.

If you need an excuse, I'm sure you'll give one. However,

"be not deceived; God is not mocked: for whatsoever a man soweth, that shall he also reap." Galatians 6:7

God is aware of our weaknesses and human frailties. He knows we make excuses. And it is for that reason that He provides us the ultimate forgiveness – Grace.

"Do what you have to do to get done what you're called to do."

Israel C. Wright, MSA, CFE, AAMS

The Problem Identified

It is written

"For the LOVE of money is the root of all evil: which while some coveted after, they have erred from the faith, and pierced themselves through with many sorrows." 1 Timothy 6:10

It is also said, "ignorance is bliss." But the most applicable quotation in the realm of prosperity would be "what you don't know can kill you." It is because of ignorance and failure to apply Christian principles (and dare I say universal principles of humanity) that many find themselves in mental anguish and financial distress. The route to solving this situation is in the saying "knowledge is power." Indeed, knowledge is the opposite of ignorance and is also the remedy for fear.

"My people are destroyed for lack of knowledge; because thou hast rejected knowledge, I will also reject thee, that thou shalt be no priest to me: seeing that thou hast forgotten the law of thy God, I will also forget my children." Hosea 4:6

That passage tells us that not only do we not know, but that we do not know because of our *own* doing. It says that we *rejected* knowledge that was readily available. How did we reject it? And what did we reject? We rejected the law of God that is instilled in each of us. We rejected the same law we are told to *'meditate therein day and night'* on, that we might have *'good success.'*

"But this shall be the covenant that I will make with the house of Israel; After those days, saith the Lord, I will put my law in their inward parts, and write it in their hearts; and will be their God, and they shall be my people." Jeremiah 31:33

What is the law? What is written in our hearts? We already identified that Jesus told us that all of the law is based on *"...love the Lord...take heed no man..."* In short, the law is love and the world is deceptive. So, if the law is in our hearts already, how do we not know it? How do we not recognize it? Why do we reject it and why don't we follow it? Remember the prince of this world? He has put in place *things* that blind and preoccupy us. These *things* keep us from seeking, learning, and practicing those principles necessary to be able to recognize and listen to our *'inward parts.'*

What are these *things*? What are those *things* that we meditate on and give our attention to instead of loving God and loving our neighbor? First, these *things* come in many forms but basically boil down to fulfilling our own desires, selfishness, greed or need. Although the motives are similar, the manifestation of these desires may vary depending on the individual. Some may desire to fit in or be envied. Some may desire glamour, happiness or security. Some individuals just desire to have an overdue bill paid! Wherever the desire originates, it generally is manifested with the acquisitions of 'bling, bling' (material items), power, or control. And whatever the desire is, generally, the way to reach of these *things* is money. After all, it is written that,

"...money answereth all things." Ecclesiastes 10:19

Consequently, in our search to fulfill our desire for 'things', we seek out money and *reject* the law that we are to uphold and obey. Honestly now; did the corporate scandals we've recently witnessed occur because the corporations involved were obeying the *'law'* or because they had a *'love of money?'*

By focusing on money, we *'pierce ourselves with sorrows.'* And we not only pierce ourselves, but anyone who is nearby. For example, if a father focuses on money, and spends his time attempting to acquire money, his child pays the price of not having much quality time with him. Or worse, the child may feel the brunt of the parent's resulting stress and frustrations. One of the many long-term effects of such a situation is that the child grows up and believes that his focus should be on money too. Thus, the child, when he becomes an adult, may do the same things that his father did. Unfortunately, the cycle continues and is perpetuated for generations. The focus on money is like a grenade; it doesn't have to hit you directly for you to feel its effects. You can be quite a distance away and still get hit by its shrapnel.

By contrast, true blessings that are received for obedience come with no such sorrows –

"The blessing of the Lord, it maketh rich, and he addeth no sorrow with it." Proverbs 10:22

It is well known that money issues are a leading cause of divorce, family tension and personal stress. But what isn't so well known is the true origin of these often-misdiagnosed symptoms. 1 Timothy 6:10 *(...the love of money...)* sums it up – searching and scrambling for that "almighty dollar" distracts and leads many down the paths of pain, agony and ruin. How did we become people who primarily focus on money?

The modern American culture is responsible for this near-sighted focus. The ideas and activities created and espoused by the world are rooted in perverted values, ignorance and/or lack of faith. Simply, it all stems from the failure to apply Biblical prosperity principles.

By glamorizing greed, selfishness and what my Army buddy Ed Connor calls 'me-ism', we have created a society of people who want to get something for nothing, who feel they 'deserve' the good things in life and who feel hurting others is okay as long as they themselves get what they want. An elaboration of the cause and tools used to create and propagate this attitude will appear in the next publication. Suffice now to say that once you grasp the principles contained herein, you will be fully able to deduct the cause and tools for yourself!

Broken down specifically, the flow of this book is dual-fold and will:

1) Illustrate what the Bible says about each of the Christian principles, and

2) Explain how to apply these principals in your daily life.

By the end of this book, you will be able to use the information within to change your perception, habits and lifestyle to achieve your most authentic and desired (and often least worked on) purpose – true prosperity.

If we look back, we will see that America was founded on Biblical principles. God is mentioned in the Constitution, Bill of Rights and (try as some may to get rid of it) the Pledge of Allegiance. It can be pointed out that "In God We Trust" is inscribed on the symbols of currency that are recognized and deemed acceptable for trade. Historic America truly believed God and put Him first in all her endeavors. And because God is a God of His word, He bestowed upon America blessings and prosperity.

"if thou shalt hearken diligently unto the voice of the Lord thy God, to observe and to do all his commandments which I command thee this day, that the Lord thy God will set thee on high above all nations of the earth:" Deuteronomy 28:1

However, God also tells us of the consequences of disobedience. *(Read Deuteronomy 28)* I am sure we can agree that America has abandoned its focus on God and we are experiencing the ramifications of doing so. Within these two directives we can deduct that God is a God of His word and will do what He says He will do.

I bring up this point not to digress into the situation of America, but rather to illustrate that obedience has its rewards and disobedience yields its consequences. America is just a visible and broad example that is a common experience we share.

Know you, Grow you. ™

Israel C. Wright, MSA, CFE, AAMS

Definition of Terms

An understanding of the terms used in the book is necessary to correctly understand the message I intend. My beliefs lead me to believe that the word of God is the Holy Bible. Although I have mostly used the King James Version *(KJV)* of the Bible to gather the most original interpretation, a few passages are from the New International Version.

I used the standard source for defining words – Webster's Dictionary. Webster's defines principle as –

1) *a basic truth, law or assumption,*

2) *a rule or standard, esp. of good behavior*

Prosperity is defined as -

1) *having success: flourishing enjoying financial security*

2) *propitious: favorable*

Obey is defined as –

1) *to carry out or yield to the command, authority, or instruction of*

2) *to carry out or comply with*

Faith is defined as -

1) *confident belief in the truth, value, or trustworthiness of a person, idea or thing.*

2) *belief not based on logical proof or material evidence.*

3) *loyalty to a person or thing*

4) *a) belief and trust in God*

b) religious conviction

5)   *a system of religious beliefs*

6)   *a set of principals or beliefs*

According to the Bible, faith is

"...the substance of things hoped for, the evidence of things not seen." Hebrews 11:1

These abstract, intangible, and often conceptual terms are used exactly as defined and mean exactly what they mean. There are no substitutions or assumptions that the reader can infer or create to appease his own ignorance or lack of belief or faith. This is not said to be egotistical or "holier-than-thou" or because I am intolerant to different religions or beliefs. Instead, it is said as a demonstration of one of the foundational principles of which you read – faith.

"But without faith it is impossible to please Him; for he that cometh to God must believe that He is, and that He is a rewarder of them that diligently seek Him." Hebrews 11:6

Just know that my intention is to empower you with the principles in a way that allows you the flexibility, creativity and freedom to use them in a manner that best suits you.

"...and this is how you come to me, without why, without power,

another link in the chain."

The Merovingian – Matrix Reloaded

Principle #1 – Acknowledging the Source

The first principle is the key one of recognizing and acknowledging that God is the source of all that exists, all that we have and all that we will ever have. We must first recognize that nothing we have belongs to us - not even our bodies! We are only stewards of God's property.

"The earth is the Lord's and the fullness thereof; the world, and they that dwell therein." Psalms 24:1

"What? know ye not that your body is the temple of the Holy Ghost, which is in you, which ye have of God, and ye are not your own?" 1 Corinthians 6:19

A frequent problem is a failure to recognize God as the source of our existence, wealth, assets and increase. Oftentimes we become full of ourselves and believe we are responsible for and created our own wealth.

"And thou say in thine heart, My power and the might of mine hand hath gotten me this wealth." Deuteronomy 8:17

How many times have you heard "Oh, I'm going to get that new (fill in the blank) with that raise (or tax return)! I deserve it!" Or to keep it simple, how about a plain "I did it!" Failing to recognize God and the power to generate wealth He has given to each of us doesn't exhibit obedience. We are commanded to,

"...remember the Lord thy God: for it is he that giveth thee power to get wealth, that he may establish his covenant which he sware unto thy fathers, as it is this day." Deuteronomy 8:18

When we do this, God has promised that he will

"cause those that love me to inherit substance; and I will fill their treasures." Proverbs 8:21

It is this acknowledgment of God as the source that creates the desire to give thanks. In turn, giving thanks creates an attitude of humility and provides an opportunity to receive continued blessings.

"In every thing give thanks: for this is the will of God in Christ Jesus concerning you." 1 Thessalonians 5:18

"And whatsoever ye do in word or deed, do all in the name of the Lord Jesus, giving thanks to God and the Father by him." Colossians 3:17

God asks that we demonstrate our thanks with tithes and offerings to Him.

"And in the process of time it came to pass, that Cain brought of the fruit of the ground an offering unto the Lord." Genesis 4:3

"Honour the Lord with thy substance, and with the firstfruits of all thine increase." Proverbs 3:9

We know the outcome of that story! But we don't have to be upset or feel rejected as Cain did. We can position ourselves to receive blessings (financial and otherwise) by simply calling God on His own word as He says to do.

"Bring ye all the tithes into the storehouse, that there may be meat in mine house, and prove me now herewith, saith the Lord of hosts, if I will not pour you out a blessing, there shall not be room enough to receive it. And I will rebuke the devourer for your sakes, and he shall not destroy the fruits of your ground; neither shall your vine cast her fruit before the time in the field, saith the Lord of hosts." Malachi 3:10-11

This is one of the key scriptures to show that tithing will be rewarded and position you to receive blessing. However, tithing is not the end all – be all that it is sometimes made out to be. Tithing alone means nothing; it must come as part of total obedience. Jesus says that tithing must be done in the proper environment and with the proper mindset.

"Woe unto you, scribes and Pharisees, hypocrites! for ye pay tithe of mint and anise and cummin, and have omitted the weightier matters of the law, judgment, mercy, and faith: these ought ye to have done, and not to leave the other undone." Matthew 23:23

To share my take on being thankful, and something that is really impressed in me, I frequently call to mind the first part of Romans 6:23 –

"for the wages of sin is death."

and another verse from Romans,

41

"for all have sinned, and come short of the glory of God."
Romans 3:23

Together, I interpret these two verses to mean that it is only by God's grace that I wake up every day. As a child of sin, the only thing that I truly "deserve" is death. No one owes me anything and if I am blessed enough to receive anything, it is because of God's grace. He indeed is my provider and I am always thankful for all that I get (be it good or bad.)

I can remember the first Army unit I was stationed in. To me, it was run very poorly by people who didn't care or have a clue. At the time, I couldn't wait to leave because I thought it was the worst place in the Army. But wait; there's more!

I thought my first unit was the worst until I went to my second one. Talk about mismanagement! I just knew that I had hit rock bottom by being stationed there. I remember often wondering what I did to deserve such a terrible place. But that's not all!

Then came Desert Storm! I went to Desert Storm with my second unit so while the unit changed quite a bit, the leadership didn't change much. It was then that I saw that my unit was a very good one – cohesive, efficient, effective. One thing took the place of my self-pity for being in such a terrible unit – Operation Desert Storm.

Believe me, war does something to a person. Being in a different county in less than peaceful conditions is disconcerting. The whole combat environment, in its mass chaos and death, appears to be artificial and thus is hard to reconcile (hence the preponderance of PTSD in combat survivors.) To come to grips and realize that you may die violently at any time is frightening. Not to mention that you may have to take another person's life; a person who is protecting his livelihood, following orders and trying to survive just as you are.

Second and more importantly, to see the desolation, hopelessness and suffering of other people really put in perspective how blessed I really was. It was upon this realization that I said to myself, "I will never say how bad I have it ever, ever again!" Those who know me have heard me tell this story and know that no matter how bad a situation I may be in, I still never think or verbalize how bad off I am. In fact, people who know me hear me say, "it could always be worse!"

The main lesson I came away with from that experience is that to be appreciative of his possessions and situation, a person must experience a time of severe lack. This may seem mean and may not apply to a select few, but overall this assessment is true. To illustrate this…

What two groups of people in the United States save money? In all my experience in the financial field, I have found that if you are a member or direct descendent of these two groups of people you are a saver. Everyone else is a spender! These two groups are depression era survivors and immigrants. Why do they save? Because they have experienced lack. Not only do they save what they have, but they also work to distance themselves from the likelihood of experiencing lack again. Unfortunately, by the third generation, the lesson of the experience has waned, and that generation is now one of spenders.

It is with this understanding that I stay ever grateful. Every day I thank God for blessing me with health, capacity, energy, and compassion. I thank Him for the insight He has given me along with the wisdom to seek Him out for myself and develop a relationship with Him.

From this, we can see that the first principle is to recognize God as the source of life and all that it contains and offers and to give thanks for it always. I believe that we must consider ourselves blessed at all times and in all situations. If we do not, we can easily fall into the trap of envy, greed and selfishness. And as you will read later (and probably already know), these characteristics destroy everything good.

- ✓ What do you do to acknowledge God daily?
- ✓ How can you demonstrate thanks more frequently?

Without gratitude, you cannot keep from being dissatisfied with things as they are.

Wallace D. Wattles

Principle #2 - Faith

Just as acknowledging God is the firm dirt that the brick is laid upon, faith is the first brick of the foundation. The second principle is that of *practicing* faith. In the Bible, faith is a common theme, that when practiced, leads to prosperity.

"But without faith it is impossible to please Him; for he that cometh to God must believe that He is, and that He is a rewarder of those that diligently seek Him." Hebrews 11:6

Please note that I write 'practicing faith', rather than just 'faith.' This is done to point out that faith must be an active action rather than a passive idea. We must do as James admonished and

"...be ye doers of the word, and not hearers only, deceiving your own selves." James 1:22

Faith is the catalyst for all action. Any action a person takes is in full belief (faith) of achieving an intended result. The car purchaser buys the car with the belief that it will run and take the person to and fro. The car thief steals the car in hopes of joyriding in it or selling it. Regardless if the act is good or evil, it still is attached to the faith that the desired outcome will be manifested.

Faith provides us strength to continue our plan. Anyone who possesses faith is capable of enduring trials, failures, and betrayals. All the mentionable people in history had faith in themselves, their beliefs, and in their actions. And unfortunately, it makes no difference if the person was good or evil. Adolph Hitler is as well-known as the Wright

Brothers. I use this extreme contrast to illustrate that the principles are indeed universal and work for whoever uses them.

"That ye be the children of your Father which is in heaven: for he maketh his sun to rise on the evil and on the good, and sendeth rain on the just and on the unjust." Matthew 5:45

However, the similarity between the good and the evil ends there. For those who were good, I believe that this faith was faith in God. Others recognized and rewarded that faith by doing what they could to assist in completing the plan. God showed His favor because the path toward kindness and giving an increase for another is in alignment with God's purpose.

For those who were evil, their faith was a faith in themselves. But as the saying goes, "no man is an island" and no individual can accomplish anything without the help of another. I am sure you have seen how people respond to someone who is selfish, exploitive, demanding, controlling and power hungry! Once that individual no longer receives assistance, his faith falters as he sees that he alone cannot control anything or anyone.

Remember this is the "prosperity" (or success) that rings true and comes to pass for those who activate the principle of faith.

In the investment field, there is the principle of "the greater the risk, the greater the potential reward." When a person invests in the stock market, he takes on a greater risk than the person who puts his money in a Certificate of Deposit at the local bank. However, the potential reward for the stock investor is likewise greater. The stock investor is aware (and believes) that he could lose all his money. But the fear and probability of losing all his money isn't as great as his faith in receiving a reward befitting his risk and patience. In contrast, the person who wants the security of knowing that he will not lose a dime (as is the case with a CD) will not (and cannot) expect a significant reward.

This, my friend, is faith at work. To use a famous figure for illustrative purposes, Thomas Edison had no tangible proof of a light bulb. It didn't exist as he envisioned it. Working to make his dream real took faith and movement outside of his comfort zone. We can imagine that he endured financial insecurity, disappointments and ridicule. He had no idea that his reward would be greater than he could have ever imagined. But just think; almost a hundred years later, his faith and actions have affected the whole world significantly.

In contrast, the person who maintains a "safe" position for fear of loss will not experience prosperity or impress his gifts upon the world in the same way. That person, while minimizing his risk, has failed to utilize his gifts and increase his worth to others. He was negligent in his duty to work and be *"fruitful and multiply."* Jesus illustrates this principle in the parable of the talents. *(Matthew 25:14-31)*

While faith is the catalyst for all action, fear often causes inaction. What do we fear? Bills getting out of hand, getting laid off, not having someone to love us, something happening to our kids – everything! My friend Bob Lord said this – "Fear of the unknown (the future) leads people to be **overly** concerned with the affairs of today." But what do we have to fear? Isn't it written

"And we know that all things work together for good to them that love God, to them who are called according to his purpose." *Romans 8:28*

47

and

"Therefore take no thought, saying, What shall we eat? Or, What shall we drink? Or, Wherewithal shall we be clothed?" Matthew 6:31

Fear is a very pervasive emotion and is the Bible's first clearly identified characteristic of sin in the Bible.

"And he (Adam) said, I heard thy voice in the garden, and I was afraid, because I was naked; and I hid myself." Genesis 3:10

When our fear overpowers our faith, we run from God and his established principles. This attempt to escape leads to a pattern of disobedience and suffering *(read the story of Jonah.)* First, our disobedience may come in the form of either failing to act or acting contrary to the principles. Second, suffering may come in the form of lack of peace, lack of blessing or very simply, death. And, just as in the case of Adam, someone other than ourselves may experience the suffering we cause. *(Read the story of Achan in Joshua 7)*

How many times has God told someone, *"Fear not?"* We must recognize that it is only with faith that we can overcome fear. Where does the faith come from?

"...faith cometh by hearing, and hearing by the word of God." Romans 10:17

This means that we must *'meditate night and day'* in the word of God to increase our faith and overcome our fears. Just like Peter, when we keep our eyes on Jesus, our faith grows so strong that we indeed can walk on water. Remember *"...with God all things are possible."* It is only when we pay attention to external factors and give credence to our surroundings and situation that we lose faith and begin to fear and thus begin to sink.

In the paratrooper community, jumping out of planes is as normal as driving a car. Even as common as jumping is, before each jump, fear made a fashionable entrance into my mind. To say that it didn't would be a lie! Although the level of fear varied, it was always present. The level varied due to visible circumstances. You can imagine how a jump into the black of night incited more fear than a jump during a sunny day. Or how a jump on a windy day caused more anxiety than a calm night jump! You may ask, "So why jump?" And I would answer, "It was necessary to accomplish the mission." It had to be done. I (along with my fellow paratroopers) believed in a higher purpose than myself, a good greater than my own life. Not jumping would put the masses in a more precarious position than a failed or fatal jump suffered by me. It sounds weird and somewhat foolish I'm sure, but believing "the sacrifice of one for the lives of many" creates the mental position necessary to develop the faith that overcomes the fear of jumping. I had faith in my tested and proven equipment (Jesus.) I had faith that my training (the Word) taught me what to do if an incident occurred (a spiritual attack, daily happenings.) I had faith in the people around me (other believers.) Overall, it was faith in each of these things that enabled me to move on and continue with the plan.

Suffice to say that I had faith in what Jesus told me;

"These things I have spoken unto you, that in me ye might have peace. In the world ye shall have tribulation: but be of good cheer; I have overcome the world." John 16:33

49

I have already been assured the victory regardless of the outcome here in on earth. This belief, this assuredness, this confidence is necessary if we are to break through the fence of fear that surrounds our comfort zone. Escaping our comfort zone is a natural by-product of our active faith and is an absolute requirement if we are to consider ourselves believers. We must remember

"for we walk by faith, not by sight." 2 Corinthians 5:7

God tells us that He will provide all our needs if we are obedient and practicing faith is an intangible form of obedience.

"...for your heavenly Father knoweth that ye have need of all these things. But seek ye first the kingdom of God, and His righteousness; and all these things shall be added unto you." Matthew 6:32-33

Because faith is working toward and for those things that are yet intangible, when it is practiced, it automatically leads to principle number three - obedience.

✓ How strong would you rate your faith?
✓ How do you plan to increase your faith?

Faith is what is left when everything else is gone.

Principle #3 – Obedience

Obedience is the mortar that secures the brinks of faith on the path to prosperity. The faith first creates our beliefs. This faith then guides our actions. The actions in turn reflect our obedience (or disobedience) of said beliefs. Thus, it can be said that obedience is nothing less than a demonstration of faith.

In the same fashion that a parent sets out limits for his child's welfare and protection, God's law is for our benefit. Although the law is not easy to apply, it is simple and its application should not be compromised. Jesus points this out when he advises

"Enter ye in at the strait gate: for wide is the gate, and broad is the way, that leadeth to destruction, and many there be which go in thereat: Because strait is the gate, and narrow is the way, which leadeth unto life, and few there be that find it." Matthew 7:13-14

The root word that is translated as strait is stenos, which means to groan. Its overall translation is difficulty. Hence, the word straitjacket. Accordingly, much like a strait jacket, the path to righteousness is difficult to navigate.

However, as negative as it appears, a strait jacket, just like the law, serves a few beneficial purposes. First, it keeps the person in it safe from hurting himself. This may be necessary as the person may not be in the right frame of mind to do for himself. Second, the strait jacket prevents him from harming others. Finally, it assists in teaching (even if by force) him restraint and control to the degree that when he is released, he can utilize his new skills and be a productive and successful contributor to his community.

Contrary to the difficult path to life, the path to destruction is referred to as broad because it is easier! Think of a straight four lane interstate highway on a clear sunny afternoon. With little traffic and clear visibility, it is a very easy road to travel. It is so easy and broad, that one can afford to drift lane to lane without significant consequence. It is so easy, a person can drive with his knees for a few miles. In fact, it is so easy, a person can fall into such a relaxing comfort zone that, as a result of his mind drifting and not saying on his purpose, he may miss his exit!

As a result of sin, and with the host of tools utilized by the world to deceive us, most people don't want to take the hard route and will take the easy way even if it means settling for less. That is why *"few there be that find it."*

So, what is the deciding factor to if we choose to obey or disobey? Of choosing the difficult route or the easy path? Pride, ego, vanity, laziness, ignorance, selfishness, desire for control – take your pick. These are the same characteristics that led to the fall of Lucifer. How often do we fall prey to wanting the easy way, thinking we know best, or wanting to be able to say that 'we' did it? When we believe

"For this is the love of God, that we keep his commandments: and his commandments are not grievous."
1 John 5:3

and

"the fear of the wicked, it shall come upon him: but the desire of the righteous shall be granted." Proverbs 10:24

we can stand strong in our faith and know that God's will for us will satisfy our desires.

Generally, an individual generally follows advice or counsel that he believes is in his best interest. For example, a child obeys his parents because he believes that they are looking out for his best interests and that they wouldn't do anything to hurt him. In essence, he trusts them. However, if the child believes he has a better alternative, he generally will ignore (disobey) the counsel and take the alternative route. So when we disobey the 'law' and all the things related to it, we are saying that we know better than God.

Have you ever ridden in an auto with a friend and he says he knows a 'shortcut' to get to where you are going? You just happen to know that the shortcut is under construction and is a more difficult path than the straight route. You insist on going the 'long way' but he insists on the 'shortcut.' Soon you two find yourselves in 'short-cut' limbo; a narrow, yellow-cone lined construction pathway to nowhere. You, as a patient and loving friend, don't want to 'go off' and give him the old 'I told you so' line, and you find that you don't have to anyway. Soon enough, he admits the error of his ways and promises next time to listen to you. Isn't this the story of disobedience in our lives?

Obedience not only guides us on the path the success for own benefit, but it also is a display of love and loyalty. Jesus says,

"If ye love me, keep my commandments." John 14:15

Let's take this further; wedding vows couples say are to "love, honor and obey." Recently the 'obey' has been disputed because it was perceived as putting one spouse in a position of subservience to the other and creating a 'leader vs. follower' hierarchy in the relationship. Each spouse felt that he/she cannot be 'less than' to his/her equal and had no intention of submitting to the other. Unfortunately, the unwillingness to submit (the desire for control?) has blinded many of us to true obedience.

I always found the phrase (and resulting dispute) odd because I see it as saying "love, love, love." Honoring and obeying someone is nothing more than loving them. I honor and obey my sister, I honor and obey my mother, I honor and obey my children.

Obedience is doing the bidding that someone requests. Is it an obligation? Is it a duty? Only if one professes love for that individual.

However, there is a situation that shows love through disobedience. This is when one knows that the request made isn't good for the person. I am sure we have seen children ask for something that isn't good for them. We, as the wise, know not to 'obey' that request, as it is detrimental for the child. However, that form of 'disobedience' is in love and stays true to the law.

The Bible has many instances of where obedience is rewarded and disobedience is punished. We can look at two Biblical men and see how the one who lacked faith and disobeyed the law did not prosper while the other who obeyed and was faithful to God did prosper.

The first man, Adam, was in the Garden of Eden and had everything provided to him.

"And God said, behold, I have given you every herb bearing seed, which is upon the face of all the earth, and every tree, in the which is the

54

fruit of a tree yielding seed; to you it shall be for meat. And to every beast of the earth, and to every foul of the air, and to every thing that creepeth upon the earth, wherein there is life, I have given every green herb for meat: and it was so." Genesis 1:29-30

For Adam, a simple act of obedience would have kept him eternally supplied and prosperous. Failure to obey this command had dire consequences and would change Adam (and mankind) forever:

"And the Lord God commanded the man, saying, Of every tree of the garden thou mayest freely eat; but of the tree of the knowledge of good and evil, thou shalt not eat of it; for in the day that thou eatest thereof thou shalt surely die." Genesis 2:16-17

It was Adam's "leaning on his own understanding" that caused him to disobey God. For whatever reason, Adam felt that his path was a better path. This disobedience led to him to losing his position in the garden, his prosperity and in the end, his life. An additional difficulty placed upon him (us) because of his lack of faith and disobedience was that the world would resist his efforts.

"...cursed is the ground because of you; through painful toil you will eat of it all the days of your life. It will produce thorns and thistles for you, and you will eat the plants of the field. By the sweat of your brow will you eat your food until you return to the ground, since from it you were taken; for dust you are and to dust you will return." Genesis 3:17-19

We can contrast the disobedience of Adam with the obedience of Job. In the story of Job, we can see how obedience pays quite handsomely! Job was a very prosperous man who had unwavering faith. Indeed, it was this faith that caused his plight! *(Job 1:1-22)* The richest man in the region who owned over 7000 sheep, 3000 camels, 500 (yoke of) oxen and 500 she asses, he

"was the greatest of all the men in the east." Job 1:3

Job, although challenged to the point of feeling futility, was blessed **because** of his faithfulness and obedience. His ignorance of the origin and purpose of his situation was significantly disturbing to him. However, it was his faithfulness and obedience that he relied upon during the difficult trial in which he lost everything (including his ten children). Through it all, while confused and hurt, Job remained faithful and obedient. And these principles, being constant and true, worked for Job.

"So the Lord blessed the later end of Job more than his beginning: for he had fourteen thousand sheep, and six thousand camels, and a thousand yoke of oxen and a thousand she asses." Job 42:12

Overall, we can see that the bonding agent for each principle is obedience.

✓ What negative consequences have you experienced because of disobedience?
✓ How much of an impact on your life have these consequences had in your life?

- ✓ Were you aware of the consequences at the time of the decision?
- ✓ Would you make the same decision again?

"And Samuel said, Hath the LORD as great delight in burnt offerings and sacrifices, as in obeying the voice of the LORD? Behold, to obey is better than sacrifice, and to hearken than the fat of rams." 1 Samuel 15:22

———————————

Principle #4 – Think It, Write It, Speak It

The fourth principle is broken down into three separate actions. These are the easiest to do, but for some, these are the most difficult. Because we haven't been taught properly, we may unintentionally be hindering our own prosperity by what we think, what we say and what we fail to annotate.

Solomon said,

"As he thinketh in his heart, so is he." Proverbs 23:7

And Paul encourages us,

"Finally, brethren, whatsoever things are true, whatsoever things are honest, whatsoever things are just, whatsoever things are pure, whatsoever things are lovely, whatsoever things are of good report; if there be any virtue, and if there be any praise, think on these things." Phillipians 4:8

We must constantly focus our minds and thoughts on those things that will guide us toward these principles. Because our deeds reflect our words, and our words are nothing less than our thoughts verbalized, maintaining a positive mental position is vital.

"A good man out of the good treasure of his heart bringeth forth that which is good; and an evil man out of the evil treasure of his heart bringeth forth that which is evil; for of the abundance of the hearth his mouth speaketh." Luke 6:45

People who first meet me are often surprised that I am a financial advisor. Their first impression is that I am a teacher or motivational speaker. This is easy to mistake because my love and focus is people and not money.

After going through the things in my life and seeing where they have led me, I have chosen to adopt these principles. As a result, my focus has changed from myself to others. I am more concerned with the growth and improvement of others rather than their (or my own) accumulation of money. Don't get me wrong; I do want a person's money to grow but I want that person to grow first. I am of the belief that a tree must be nourished, protected and cultivated before it will produce good fruit. Likewise, it is necessary for an individual to grow personally before he can expect his money to grow.

How does one grow personally? Personal growth is achieved by expanding your thinking and accepting new ideas. I am sure you know a person who is stuck in a personal rut. That person just refuses to see or do something different. Not that something different is truly there, but oftentimes it is just the perception that needs to be altered. For example, someone who has gone through a bitter divorce may choose to blame the other person for wrecking his life. He may linger on and on about it and allow it to fester and grow until it becomes a sort of cancer. And we know what cancer does.

But if he were to change his perception of the divorce from a painful experience to an opportunity for a new start or as a learning experience, he can sooner focus his energy on a new plan and a new path toward success.

The second part of the fourth principle is something practiced by many "successful" people. In our daily lives, we frequently think of

59

things we would like to do. We ponder on these ideas and try to figure them out. Sometime, however, the ideas pass and we never quite figure them out. This makes it nearly impossible to work toward making the ideas come to pass. Generally, we can prevent the loss of our ideas by writing them down.

In the field of psychology, studies of the mind and behavior must be codified in order to be measured. Asking an abstract question such as, "how happy are you?" must be positioned in a manner for measurement. That is why some polls have gauges such as "on a scale of one to five." This codification is the same as writing down your thoughts in that they become visible, tangible, and measurable.

Just like God breathed life into Adam when he was yet a shell of a body, we too should seek to breathe life into our ideas. Thoughts and ideas are intangible and abstract and must made tangible for them to be realized. And the way to do that is to write them down. We can give our ideas the chance to live when we transform them from ideas to visions. How? Ideas, once written, become visions. Writing our thoughts and ideas down provide the opportunity to meditate on them and creates a receptive environment for the Holy Spirit to speak to us about them. It is the Holy Spirit who breathes the life into our ideas and embodies them as visions. Then as visions, something we perceive as alive, our ideas take on a life of their own and we work toward sustaining their lives and preventing their deaths.

As a financial advisor, I have created quite a few financial plans. Each financial plan lists the client's current situation, resources and goals. I must add that this is *not* unique to financial planning! Every person in his or her profession, career or just plain daily living implements such a tool to 'keep his eyes on the prize.' It is with this information that a system of approach is created to accomplish the objectives. Such a plan also provides additional benefits: a way of managing activity and a gauge to review the current status.

Because the plan is a path that leads toward an objective yet to be achieved, we should expect the need to modify the plan due to changes in current and foreseeable situations. However, although the plan is modified, the objective remains the same. We must recognize and believe, regardless of the changes in the plan or situation, that by holding steadfast to the objective, it will be achieved. When we hold tight to this belief, we can eliminate the worry and fear we are sure to experience along the way. It is written,

"And the Lord answered me, and said, Write the vision, and make it plain upon tables, that he may run that readeth it. For the vision is yet for an appointed time, but at the end it shall speak, and not lie: though it tarry, wait for it; because it will surely come, it will not tarry."
Habakkuk 2:2-3

Think of a grocery list. I have a list on my refrigerator that I maintain and write things for when I discover something I need to purchase on my next visit to the grocery store. Because I can more easily recall what I wrote down, I do not really need even to take the list with me. The list is written in two places – on the paper and in my head. I can visualize the list on the refrigerator easily. The print is calling me out by making me stay true and manifesting the idea.

Writing an idea down gives it life and makes it real. Both writing and reading your ideas stimulate thought and create an opportunity and environment for reflection. And it is during this quasi meditation time

61

that God's spirit comes in and provides you the insight to be creative and visualize potential problems and barriers and provide their solutions.

I am a testament to this activity. Recently I discovered a tablet I had written in six years ago. In the tablet, I wrote a list of objectives that I wanted to accomplish. Each of the objectives was something I needed to further expand my knowledge to assist others in the financial field. At the time I rediscovered the list, six out of the seven things on the list had been accomplished. And indeed, six years later, you are the beneficiary of those activities as you read this book. As for that seventh objective - it no longer applied to my situation and was not necessary to complete.

I was truly surprised to find that list and to reread it. It brought a smile to my face and I just shook my head and praised God.

Those who know me know that I have journals from 1992 that lay out the things that I wanted to achieve and become in my career. If you read the back cover of this book, each one of those things that I have acquired (and become) was in my journal.

The last principle has been mentioned already. That of *"calling those things which be not as though they were."* As a financial advisor, I encounter many people who always talk about how little money they have and how poor they are. Believe me, I get this all day! "Man, I can't afford to invest now." Or "I can't afford life insurance." These people are telling the truth and honestly see their situation as real. But what they don't see is that they create (or at least prolong) their situation by what they say. Speech is power; what you get is a direct result of what you say!

James tell us,

"But above all things, my brethren, swear not, neither by heaven, neither by the earth, neither by any other oath: but let your yea be yea; and your nay, nay; lest ye fall into condemnation." James 5:12

And Solomon teaches us,

"Death and life are in the power of the tongue; and they that love it shall eat the fruit thereof." Proverbs 18:21

Jesus taught this principle very clearly. There are two principles within the following verses. The first is that of speech. We can see that "say" or "said" is in this passage four times.

*"Have faith in God. For verily I **say** unto you, that whosoever shall **say** unto this mountain, be thou removed, and be thou cast into the sea; and shall not doubt in his heart, but shall believe that those things which he **saith** shall come to pass, he shall have whatsoever he **saith**." Mark 11:22-23*

Also notice that it says, *"not doubt."* This goes back to the principle of faith. If doubt exists in your heart, there can be no faith. But faith must be practiced. It has a partner - work. This is because faith and any form of action go hand in hand. James wrote,

"...faith without works is dead also." James 2:26

When I was getting out of the Army, my sergeant major asked what I was going to do when I got out 'in the world.' I told him I was going to become a financial and life coach. He just chuckled in disbelief. But I believed it with all I had. All glory to God, with the 'measure of faith' I had been given and by speaking on it, writing it down, and working for it, I am.

So, principal number four empowers us to create the outcome: Think it, Write it, Speak it.

✓ Are your thoughts in line with the law and the will of God?
✓ Do you write down your goals?
✓ Do you speak positively of the things you wish to accomplish?
✓ Think of an instance of something you've said that later came to pass. Was it good or bad?

Man's mind, once stretched by a new idea, never regains its

original dimension.

Oliver Wendell Holmes

Principle #5 – Work

God Himself is a working God. His labor is described in the very first verse of the Bible -

"In the beginning, God <u>created</u> the heaven and the earth."
Genesis 1:1

The principle of work is primary in that it is the manifestation of the acknowledgment of and faith in the principles. We've identified that James said we cannot just believe and have faith without acting upon that belief and faith. Remember, that God put Adam in the Garden of Eden with a purpose:

"The Lord God took the man and put him in the Garden of Eden to <u>work</u> it and take care of it." Genesis 2:15

Let's look at that again. God put Adam in the Garden of Eden with a purpose – work! Contrary to popular understanding, work was not the punishment Adam suffered for his disobedience. It is written, *"the wages of sin is death."* So <u>death</u>, not work, was introduced to the world because of disobedience. Work was already part of the sinless order. If work was assigned by God *<u>prior</u>* to the fall of man and the onset of sin, then we know that it is God's will that we work and that work isn't just a result of sin. Jesus confirms this when He tells us that the key to the kingdom is the principle of sowing and reaping. *(read Mark 4)*

"and he said to them, Know ye not this parable? And how then will ye know all parables?" Mark 4:12

This is the principle that is frequently ignored. We all know that person who wants to get something for nothing. He wants the reward but doesn't want to put forth the work. He wants the income of a doctor but doesn't want to go through the demanding rigors of medical school! He wants the raise but not the responsibility demanded of it. Personally, I feel that our society has a real problem with this issue.

Before any of us can expect any harvest, we must first plant the seed. Any of us who plant, do so in full expectation and faith of a time of reaping. In addition to the act of faith, planting itself takes work. I started my tax business with the faith that if I knew the subject and was honest and treated people well, then it would grow and prosper.

But harvesting doesn't end at planting. It continues with the nurturing, the cultivating, the weeding, the protecting. As an example, in my business, I kept up with the laws and the changes and genuinely became friends with my clients. And, boy oh boy, you can believe that I put forth time, energy, and even finances that I didn't always have readily available to make the vision come to pass.

And last of all comes the harvest. And the harvest itself is work! To me, this book is my harvest. I get to share what I have learned in my trials and doings with others so that they may benefit. And believe me, this book was a true **_labor_** of love! Thus, in all we do, we must take note that our work never ends.

When I told my sister of this revelation while I was writing this book, she said, "Wow. That makes me feel better." And to be honest, it made me feel better too.

Now I am not saying that everyone is lazy and everyone tries to scheme out of working. That isn't true and that isn't what I am saying. Most people are hard workers and wouldn't know what to do if they didn't work! I am just pointing out that work doesn't have to be looked at as a chore. It can instead be looked at as internally fulfilling and our individual contribution to our fellow man. I am sure you know a few people who love what they do. And the reason they love it is because they don't look at it as work; they honestly see it as fulfilling and as a blessing.

Again, we can identify that the "world" instills in us a disdain for work and creates in us a desire to escape from it. Think of how we are bombarded with the idea of "retirement." All the while it is made more and more difficult to do. (I say this from the perspective of a financial advisor.) As long as we have an attitude of "I Deserve" or "It's my right" and fail to work for whatever we seek, then we negate the principles and reap the consequences of disobedience.

We must realize that work is our lot in life and it enables us to provide for our families and ourselves. According to the author of Ecclesiastes, enjoying the benefits (or fruits) of our labor is a gift from God.

"Every man also to whom God hath given riches and wealth, and hath given him power to eat thereof, and to take his portion, and to rejoice in his labour; this is the gift of God." Ecclesiastes 5:19

The word of God clearly warns of the result of not working and of being idle and slothful - poverty.

"Yet a little sleep, a little slumber, a little folding of the hands to sleep: so shall thy poverty come as one that travelleth, and thy want as an armed man." Proverbs 6:10-11

Remember the *"kill, steal, and destroy?"* mission of the prince of this world? Consider this…In our country, the employment rate of some men (varying by age, income-level, race) has fallen significantly from decades ago. Whereas in the past, "men were men," current men are frequently deemed "less than men." Employment (or contribution to the whole) is critical to an individual's self-esteem and mental/emotional health. Psychological studies show that unemployment may cause men to respond by engaging in maladaptive behaviors – alcohol and drug abuse, promiscuity, anger, hostility, aggression, apathy, and depression. These are normal responses when people do not feel engaged, valued, fulfilled, or as if they are contributing. Thus, we have a great number of single mothers and children growing up without fathers. And the situation of "absentee fathers" causes adverse environments that generate maladapted children and negative attitudes towards men. One common effect of this for all involved is the distraction the situation causes. From that comes a failure to identify one's internal essence (spirit) and the overall disconnection from the Most High. I venture to say that the increased unemployment among men is not by accident but is created intentionally to facilitate these byproducts.

The social narrative that work is bad may cause people to avoid work. And this avoidance may be why so many do not prosper. The lost and unaware would prefer to just sit back and wait for the reward because they feel they "deserve" it or even feel they have done enough to earn it.

I am sure you have heard or seen that employee who had the attitude of "I don't get paid enough to do this." This is an attitude that contradicts the principles. We must consider that in most employment situations, the worker and the employer agree on the wages to be paid and the tasks to be done. If the worker ever feels that the value of his effort exceeds his wage, he should remember that the employer is not obligated to pay *above* the agreed upon wage. The employee indeed is only due his agreed upon wage. *(Read Matthew 20:1-16)*

This is why a person can be passed over for a promotion he feels he has earned. The person doing the promoting didn't feel that the work was sufficient. The work could have been accomplished in a spirit of greed, or resentment or laziness; all of which decrease the value of the contributed energy and the accomplishment. I know (for some) this statement leaves a lot of room for debate due to human conditions and inequalities. But we know that the principles remain true to those who activate them. Solomon spoke about these potential inequalities and told those in positions of power,

"Withhold not good from them to whom it is due, when it is in the power of thine hand to do it. Say not unto thy neighbor, Go, and come again, and tomorrow I will give; when thou hast it by thee." Proverbs 3: 27-28

So, if we *"faint not"* in doing our work (and practicing our faith), our reward will come. Sometimes it may even come from those who would prefer not to have us rewarded! Why? Because it is written –

"For promotion cometh neither from the east, nor from the west, nor from the south, But God is the judge: he putteth down one, and setteth up another." Psalms 75:6-7

I know you have seen or experienced someone who begrudgingly gave a reward to someone whom they had rather not. That person in the position of rewarding was determined to not reward (for whatever reason) the individual for the work done. But what that boss forgot was that the reward was not a gift! It was earned fair and square! It was _"Due"_! It was a bill, a debt, an obligation that _had_ to be paid! No matter what the boss's feelings were, the reward was going to be given. It just so happened that he was the tool that God used to reward the faith and work.

We must recognize that work is an individual principle. With all the different people on this planet, and their varying degrees of talent, intelligence and skill, there is no way we can measure an equitable level of work tit-for-tat. Unfortunately, we frequently fall prey to the irrelevant and unreasonable comparison of what we do in relation to what others do, what we have to what others have or how much we have to how much others have. Because we are all different and judged according to our own faithfulness to God, it is absolutely useless as well as counterproductive to compare ourselves to another person.

Comparing is the one of the most cascading, pervasive and self-destructive acts we do. For instance, let's say my son, Andrew, has a friend whose parents bought him a new video game console. What would happen if Andrew comes homes to me and asks me to buy him a similar console because his friend's parents bought him one? When I tell Andrew no, and explain to him the concept of work, true need and "garbage in, garbage out", I do so with the intent of teaching him valuable lessons he will understand, accept and practice. But what if he doesn't? What if he feels upset towards me, unloved by me, resentful of his friend and angry overall? These counterproductive emotions occurred all because he used someone else's situation as a barometer for his own. In every instance, the result of comparing leaves us either with a feeling of inadequacy or superiority, both of which create an attitude that is counter to working and giving our all.

Think of advertisements and social media; are there greater illustrations of tools of distractions, deceptions and influences for comparing?

Do you know what the result of the first recorded comparison after the fall was? Death! Cain killed Abel when he compared what he received from God to what Abel received. Cain failed to obey God and felt that although he cut corners, he should have received the full benefit and acceptance that Abel did for following the letter of the law. Rather than compare his result to Abel's, Cain should have reevaluated what he did and taken note on how he could have improved it in God's eyes; indeed, those are the only eyes that matter. In other words, apply the principles and know that God is the only judge. Know that He judges us all by what we ourselves do in relation to His will; not in relation to what others do.

Here is another point to remember about the principle of work. In today's world, because our society is based on commerce and trade, it is unlikely that our labor directly produces our reward. For example, in the old days, a farmer could potentially feed himself and his family by his own hands. At least he could do that; many of us today aren't in that position (and would starve if we were!) However, even then that is all that he could do! He still had to have a home and clothes and shoes. So how does he get those things? Unless he did those things too, he gets those things through trade - by exchanging the fruits of his labor for someone else's fruit.

Now I want you to think as a purchaser. When you are searching for a product or a service to fulfill a need that you have, what causes you to choose one vendor over another? For most people, it is the perceived quality, reliability and overall value for the price paid. And most people are willing to pay more for such qualities. If they weren't, then Mercedes Benz would go out of business tomorrow because everyone would buy a simple, functional, inexpensive car!

The point of this example is to illustrate that generally our reward comes from another source. And that other person's willingness to give us our fair "due" is based on our integrity, our reliability, and the value we offer. We have seen this when someone says "I've been keeping my eyes on you and you do good work." or "I wouldn't take my business anywhere else!" or "If you ever move, you let me know, because I am following you!" This dedication and loyalty from others is because of your identified good name. When I was a kid, my mother always told me, "The only thing you have is your name." And she was right; it is written,

"A good name is rather to be chosen than great riches, and loving favour rather than silver and gold." Proverbs 22:1

Your name is vitally important. If you were a farmer, and was known as a liar, a cheat, a thief or a slacker, what is the likelihood others would purchase your goods? They would feel that your personal traits reflected in your goods and would spend their money elsewhere. So that farmer might have harvested a ton of food, but he may not have a storehouse for it. What about his shoes? How effective could a shoeless-farmer be? A barefooted farmer wouldn't get much done.

The social viewpoint is that your name is tied fundamentally to your work ethic. And the quality of your work is how one gets positioned for recognition, promotions or those exclusive cases or clients. A person cannot promote himself! It is always through another's observation of your attitude, loyalty, dedication, or discipline that you are given the opportunity to do more and to be more. You can tell which people recognize this fact by what they say when they are given accolades. If they say, "I'd like to thank my employees (fans, coworkers), because without them I wouldn't be here," then they know. However, if they focus on themselves, they just may be in for a soon-to-come rude awakening and tumultuous experience.

Lastly, the principle of work must be in accordance with God's will and the purpose He has for you. If the work you do is not within the parameters of obedience to the *'law'*, the work is detrimental and its results create a chasm that must be bridged in the future. This 'catching up' is the stuff regret, and shoulda', coulda' and woulda' are made of. This catching up is an additional burdensome work that 'coulda' been prevented with obedience. David tells us,

"Except the Lord build the house, they labour in vain that build it: except the Lord keep the city, the watchman waketh but in vain." Psalms 127:1

Overall, work comes in different forms and degrees, and is an individual contribution and effort designed to benefit everyone. And although our own hand oftentimes does not produce our own reward, be mindful that work is always responsible for our increase.

✓ Do you try to take the 'easy way' or the 'short cut' in the things you do?

73

✓ Do you have an 'I DESERVE' mentality? If so, why?

✓ How hard are you willing to work and what are you willing to sacrifice to achieve your purpose?

Work is love made visible.

Kahlil Gibran

Principle #6 - Patience

The running partner of work is patience. I have been told by more than one person that this principle is the one *"I need help with."* As mentioned before, all things are done in expectation of something in return. But frequently, if we do not receive what we expected _when_ we expect it, we get frustrated and begin to lose faith. Since *"faith without works is dead,"* the principle of patience is an act of practicing faith. First off, let's identify that practicing patience is not the same as delaying or procrastinating.

"But if we hope for that we see not, then do we with patience wait for it." Romans 8:25

Patience encompasses the subsets of self-control, self-discipline, resilience, determination and perseverance. These characteristics have an objective that is very similar for everyone. For example, my level of self-control may have to be greater because I am more prone to outbursts. However, it should produce the same objective as yours – no outbursts. Another subset of patience, determination, is the same for everyone – we practice determination until the goal is met.

Patience also has individual characteristics. This type of patience is an individual's ability to withstand noise and external factors in order to allow the necessary components of the completion process to naturally occur. This is where my patience may be different than yours due to our personality and temperament differences. My older brother has frequently told me I move too quickly and don't sit back and think things out. In *his* eyes and for *his* character I move fast. But to me, I am very patient and move at the right pace without forcing or procrastinating. And in turn, I think he moves way too slowly! But even as different as our styles are, mine works for me and his works for him. Over time and with experience, maturity and tuning in to the Holy Spirit, we have both learned to appreciate and incorporate each other's styles into our own lives as the situation dictates.

Because the Holy Spirit knows our personality, our strengths, our weaknesses and our tolerances, He relates to us differently – much like a parent does with each of her children. Our responsibility is twofold: create, tune and maintain our spiritual awareness for us to know when the Holy Spirit is calling; and develop the faith so we can act without regard to fear.

It is easy to see how critical it is that we maintain a connection and awareness of our spiritual selves because it provides an avenue for the inner spirit to guide us to act at the proper time. Remember that we are to 'meditate therein day and night' on the law for us to experience 'good success.' (again, frequency and proximity.)

If we fail to create and maintain a connection, we fail to develop the faith necessary to have full trust in God. We then fall prey to acting in our own perception of time and according to our own will. Solomon told us to,

"Trust in the LORD with all thine heart; and lean not unto thine own understanding." Proverbs 3:5

If we fail to obey the guidance of the Holy Spirit and act on His timetable, we open the door to premature activity and tend to make hasty decisions that often result in negative consequences.

"A faithful man shall abound with blessings: but he that maketh haste to be rich shall not be innocent...he that hasteth to be rich hath an evil eye, and considereth not that poverty shall come upon him." Proverbs 28:20, 22

Also,

"The thoughts of the diligent tend only to plenteousness; but of every one that is hasty only to want." Proverbs 21:5

Our level of patience dictates our outcome. It is because of impatience that Esau traded his birthright to Jacob for a bowl of soup! You can read that story for yourself to learn of the dramatic results we all suffer to this day. *(Genesis 25)* Our level of patience also dictates how we perceive our trials.

"My brethen, count it all joy when ye fall into divers temptations; Knowing this, that the trying of your faith worketh patience. But let patience have her perfect work, that ye may be perfect and entire, wanting nothing." James 1:2-4

Someone with more patience may be calmer, less stressed and clearheaded enough to still activate the principles. Someone with immature patience only sees his situation before him and makes hasty decisions.

Oftentimes the results from the actions made with a hasty decision are worse than the problem we were trying to solve. Have you ever left the "busy" checkout line only to have the cash register you moved to run out of receipt paper? *And* the person ahead of you is writing a check and

77

can't find his identification. _And_ out of the corner of your eye, you see the person who was behind you in the first line push her overflowing cart out of the door! _And_ just as you jet out of the parking lot, you rear end the car ahead of you because you were blinded by anger. This *"things just get worse"* domino effect is the common path of impatience.

If we truly love and trust the Lord,

"We know that all things work together for good to them that love God, to them who are the called according to his purpose." Romans 8:28

Exhibiting patience does take a committed effort. But it is necessary if we wish to fully obey and activate the principles. We must *"fight the good fight"* and continue until the appointed time. (Be aware that we may not live to see the appointed time!) We have identified already that our reward is promised - but not without a requirement.

*"And let us not be weary in well doing: for in due season we shall reap, if we **faint** not."* Galatians 6:9

Many times, we see others benefit and live 'prosperously' while we observe and believe that they are not obeying the principles. It is important that we do not let this cloud our vision and prevent us from following the principles. Feeling that we are not getting our reward may discourage us and we may cease our work prematurely.

We must learn to be satisfied with what we have and become good stewards and managers of what we have been blessed with. When we demonstrate these things, we open the door to then be entrusted with more. Jesus pointed this out when He said,

"He that is faithful in that which is least is faithful also in much; and he that is unjust in the least is unjust also in much. If therefore ye have not been faithful in the unrighteous mammon, who will commit to your trust the true riches?" Luke 16:10-11

Young children are notorious for their impatience. One of the reasons they are impatient is because they are unaware of the future and as a result, live in the "now." For example, I may tell my daughter to go put on her shoes and get in the car. The first thing out of her mouth is "where are we going?" Is that a valid concern? The question she asks enables me to see that her focus isn't on the task at hand (putting on her shoes and going outside) but instead on something that she has no information about. I then find myself having to remind her to tie her shoes properly and take her time. I must now spend time making sure she does the first task completely and correctly. All because her mind is drifting from her given and known task to the next step of which she is totally unaware.

Don't we do that? Don't we want to know the total picture before we act on the first step? Why do we do that? As my daughter's loving father, I would never do anything to hurt her. I would never lie to her or lead her astray. Everything that I do with her or for her will be to her benefit. And I am a man filled with frailties and flaws. If I do that as an earthly father, how much more can our heavenly Father take care of us? Jesus said,

*"If ye then, being **evil**, know how to give good gifts unto your children, how much more shall your **Father** which is in heaven give good things to them that ask him?" Matthew 7:11*

The assignments He gives us are just enough to keep us focused on the task at hand. The result has already been planned for our good. We already have the victory, my friend.

Unfortunately, most of us lack faith. We act as if we don't trust God. We believe in the lie that the world has told us - - "if you want something done right, do it yourself." This desire for independence and control comes from our sinful flesh and manifests in our emotions. As our feelings take precedence over our thoughts and logic, doubt seeps in and erodes our faith. We can prevent this by maintaining a vigilant awareness of our emotions and their origin. Doing this allows us to keep our thoughts paramount and in line and protects them from the effects of reactive and rampant feelings. It is written

"Keep thy heart with all diligence; for out of it are the issues of life." Proverbs 4:23

I can think of just about every emotionally based decision I've made. Talk about issues of life! I found that when I *'leaned on my own understanding'* I encountered more issues than I expected. We must guard our emotions (heart), because when we act upon them or seek to fulfill them, we tend to get more than we bargain for and less than we desire.

My friend, patience cannot exist without faith and impatience is rooted in fear. So, to eliminate impatience we must eliminate fear. And faith kills them both! Since we know that James tells us that *trials* increase our patience, it may not be wise to seek patience. I interpret what James writes to mean that if I pray for patience, the way I receive it comes in the form of more trials. Don't pray for patience; instead increase your faith! We all have been given a *'measure of faith;'* it is our responsibility to develop it.

We can eliminate impatience and increase our faith by seeking God and trusting Him to do those things He says He will do. We know that He will neither *"leave nor forsake"* us, so what is there to fear? As we recognize and stay in tune with His will for us, we will position ourselves to stay tuned to the guiding hand of the Holy Spirit and let His timing become our own.

✓ What is the longest time you waited for something you really wanted?
✓ Did that desire have an objective in alignment with God's law?
✓ What are you waiting for now? How much longer are you willing to wait?

Comprehension is not a requisite for cooperation.

Dr. Cornell West (The Matrix Reloaded)

Principle #7 ~ Benevolence

Benevolence is the principle that encompasses more than any other. This is where the proverbial rubber hits the road. This is the one that most of us fail to recognize or activate.

Because of sin, each of us seeks to fulfill our selfish desires, our greed and our lusts. In this search of selfish realization, we neglect the second part of the law – *"love thy neighbor as thyself."* We can witness this greed every day in the attitudes and actions of people - -

"Me first!"

"What have you done for me lately?" or

"I'ma gets mines!" <sic>

More importantly, to illustrate that this attitude can be wholly pervasive and that none of us is beyond its reach, these phrases are uttered every day in some form or another by people of varying backgrounds and education levels. Harboring, cultivating and activating a selfish attitude creates an environment that cannot simultaneously foster those things necessary for the principles to operate successfully. What does that mean? That means that greed and selfishness quickly and completely negate all the principles and their ensuing benefits.

When we strive to fulfill the law of putting God first and our neighbor second, we automatically activate the principles that bring about prosperity. Remember it is written,

"But seek ye first the kingdom of God, and his righteousness; and all these things shall be added unto you." Matthew 6:33

But how do we know that this is true and works? King Solomon is known for his wisdom and wealth. But how did he acquire such notoriety? It all started with a benevolent request. When God visited Solomon in a dream and asked *"...what shall I give thee..."*, Solomon replied from his heart,

"Give me now wisdom and knowledge, that I may go out and come in before this people; for who can judge this thy people, that is so great?" 2 Chronicles 1:10

The reward that Solomon received for his benevolent act was not only the wisdom he requested, but also riches beyond his own comprehension.

"...and I will give thee riches, and wealth, and honour, such as none of the kings have had that have been before thee, neither shall there any after thee have the like." 2 Chronicles 1:12

Solomon's wealth, which has yet to be matched by anyone, was bestowed upon him because he did not seek it! He placed other's welfare ahead of his own and sought only to acquire the necessary resources to guide and lead God's people in a way that most benefited them. My friend, benevolence will yield returns like the stock market never has and never will!

There are many ways to define benevolence. But for the purposes of the principles and obeying the *law*, benevolence means anything that you think, do or say that improves, increases, or benefits someone other than yourself. These benefits are not always immediate but may also be long-term and possibly permanent. To sum it up, benevolence is the display of Paul's characteristics of love in 1 Corinthians 13.

These characteristics in today's world include candor, integrity, honesty, and community. Benevolence also includes teaching, correcting, guiding, motivating, informing and serving others. Paul tells us that we must not be selfish and vain, but instead be humble and regard others higher than ourselves.

"Let nothing be done through strife or vainglory; but in lowliness of mind let each esteem other better than themselves. Look not every man on his own things, but every man also on the things of others."
Phillipians 2:3-4 (NIV)

You may wonder how these characteristics fit under benevolence. Remember that Jesus' command is to *"love thy neighbor as thyself."* This is different from the Golden Rule that espouses "Treat others the way you want to be treated." The Golden Rule is a fallacy and here is an explanation why.

Let's suppose I prefer conversation and social interaction. Let's suppose that you are the opposite and prefer being alone. If, when we first meet, I attempt to get you to converse and be social, it may create disharmony between us. Overall, I should not treat another the way I want to be treated because he may not like what I like. True benevolence is when I treat another in the way *he* would like to be treated. To do this requires that I pay attention to him, listen to him, learn him. This is a tedious process (which may be why it is so infrequently done) but the reward is great. And anyone who loves another is willing to spend the time and energy required to develop such an understanding.

When I love you as I love myself, I am honest with you. I am straightforward with you. I want to help you. Benevolence, indeed, is each of these things.

Be mindful that kind deeds done for your family members are not true benevolence. Jesus says,

"For if ye love them which love you, what reward have ye? Do not even the publicans the same?" Matthew 5:46

Jesus tells of the reward we receive when we practice genuine benevolence.

"Then shall the King say unto them on his right hand, Come, ye blessed of my Father, inherit the kingdom prepared for you from the foundation of the world; For I was an hungered, and ye gave me meat: I was thirsty, and ye gave me drink: I was a stranger, and ye took me in: Naked, and ye clothed me: I was sick, and ye visited me: I was in prison, and ye came unto me." Matthew 25:34-36

Unfortunately, few people have the time or money to do such kind deeds. I believe that the system of this world has designed it so we would have little time, money, or other resources to do these deeds and be obedient to the principles.

Having "extra" money may not be necessary to do good deeds, but a little bit of effort and restructuring of our time will suffice. I believe that the principle of benevolence does not call for an extreme act of generosity. Benevolence is a little deed of kindness for a stranger. It is the chastising of the young man spray painting graffiti on the wall. It is telling the friend that he is wrong even though you sympathize with his hurt. It is not being wasteful. It is not throwing cigarette butts out of the window while driving. It is helping the disabled person tie her shoe. It is driving your SUV a little to the right so the car behind you can see. It is listening to that elderly person on the bus who is just talking away and telling her life story. It is simply looking at and genuinely feeling life through the eyes of the person you are with.

Referring to that toddler again, we can take a few characteristics from him to show that he too is naturally benevolent. He wants to be helpful, he wants to give, he wants to please. It isn't until he learns fear and the idea of mortality (temporary existence) that he begins the infamous "Mine!" mantra.

However, if the toddler *believes* that he will get something of value in return (the same item or not), he will gladly relinquish the item. That is human nature! Each of us daily gives up something in expectation of something in return. We go to work; we give up our time in expectation of money. We go to the movies; we give up money in expectation of entertainment. I am not saying that we only give to get something tangible in return. That isn't true. I may dedicate some of my time to my daughter and the only thing I expect to receive is a feeling of happiness as I spend time with her. I give my son lessons that I have learned in expectation that he will learn from them and not go through what I did. We give love in expectation of receiving happiness and joy and satisfaction in doing so.

However, there is always a possibility that we give those things and never receive what we expected. The company we work for may go broke and leave its employees hanging. The movie we pay to see is disappointing and does not entertain at all. The love we give may be unrequited and leave us heartbroken. So, we can see that it is always because we expect something in return that any of us give. Faith is the anchor than we all tie our expectations to and it is only through faith that benevolence can ever truly exist.

It was identified in the last chapter that fear is the root of impatience. But that isn't the only characteristic fear influences. Fear also stifles benevolence. If we believe that we are made in the image of God, then it stands to reason that we are a giving species. Just as a toddler's natural desire to give and help is clearly visible, so it is in adults. Our desire to give does not die in our youth.

How many times have you driven down the highway and seen someone in need? Haven't you seen someone with a car problem, or someone who needs a ride? Doesn't your heart reach out to that person in his plight? Don't you truly want to stop and give assistance? Is it because you fear for yourself (and those with you) that you don't stop and help? Is it because you fear the loss of your time? Or is it because you fear your plans being disrupted that prevent you from assisting this person so obviously in need? Again, fear prevents the principles from being activated. But we should remember,

"The fear of man bringeth a snare: but whoso putteth is trust in the Lord shall be safe." Proverbs 29:25

Benevolence also includes the traditional giving to the poor. Because it is through work that we earn and the ability to earn is a blessing, we must remember those who are less fortunate. You can rest assured that when you are benevolent, all your needs will be taken care of.

"What is it, Lord? The angel answered, Your prayers and gifts to the poor have come up as a memorial offering before God." Acts 10:4

"Give, and it shall be given unto you; good measure, pressed down, and shaken together, and running over, shall men give into your bosom. For with the same measure that ye mete withal it shall be measured to you again." Luke 6:38

For clarification, the principle of benevolence is different from the tithing and offering. Benevolence is to and for anyone other than yourself while tithing and offering are to God as a form of acknowledgment and thanks.

It must be mentioned that benevolence cannot be done for glamour or recognition because *"God is not mocked,"* and also because it negates the reward:

"Take heed that ye do not your alms before men, to be seen of them: otherwise ye have no reward of your Father which is in heaven." Matthew 6:1

Service to others is an integral part of benevolence. Service, like obedience, is a form of love. Jesus demonstrated this when he washed the feet of his disciples. *(Read John 13:5)* True service to another can only be done when one is steadfast and firm in his beliefs and position. This occurs as a result of knowing one's purpose. Peter protested Jesus washing his feet because he knew that Jesus was a higher being than he.

But Jesus had no such issues. It was because Jesus knew Himself that He was able to "stoop" to the level of washing a sinner's feet. This confidence is something that is attained through wisdom.

Wisdom comes as a result of the four key activities that I believe we were created for. This wisdom is a crucial ingredient to success as it provides us the key ingredients necessary for our decisions and it establishes the limits of our behavior. These four things are – worshiping, learning, growing and teaching.

The first, worshipping, is uniquely towards and for God. Worship is a natural human need; God put the desire in us. We know this to be true because God Himself warns us of the dangers of worshipping anything other than Him. Worshipping is an affirmation of our acknowledgement of God and establishes a foundation of trust, hierarchy and dependence that sets the tone for our personal development and overall success.

The second and third purposes are self-related. The second purpose, learning, is an individual process whereas we seek completion, fulfillment and answers. Our beliefs, values and personal ethics are direct reflections of our learning. This learning is comprised of the mistakes, the heartbreaks, and the betrayals that we experience. David wrote,

"It is good for me that I have been afflicted; that I might learn thy statutes. The law of thy mouth is better unto me than thousands of gold and silver." Psalms 119:71-72

Just as there is no right without wrong, there can be no joy without the existence of pain. As a result of our painful experiences, failures and disappointments commingling with the joys we encounter with our families, achievements and successes, we learn and develop insight. Both types of experiences are designed to lead us to find our God-given purpose and drive us to fulfilling it. We obey the law by default when we identify our purpose and act towards fulfilling it.

Growing, purpose number three, is increased as a result of learning (from our experiences). God instituted our natural desire to grow when He commanded that everything *'be fruitful and multiply.'* This growing can be mental, physical, spiritual or social. Overall, growing bring us closer in harmony with the Most High, increases self-awareness, and increases empathy and understanding for others. The increase we obtain (and retain) is referred to as wisdom. Paul wrote,

"When I was a child, I spake as a child, I understood as a child, I thought as a child: but when I became a man, I put away childish things." 1 Corinthians 13:11

The fourth purpose, teaching, deals with our relationships with others. Jesus was a teacher, and if we are to emulate Him, we too should teach those things that are of God.

"There was a man of the Pharisees, named Nicodemus, a ruler of the Jews: The same came to Jesus by night, and said unto him, Rabbi, we know that thou art a teacher come from God: for no man can do these miracles that thou doest, except God be with him." John 3:1-2

Teaching is the passing on of the wisdom we have attained. This is an act of selflessness and benevolence and completes our purpose on this earth.

Personally, I refer to this as the *LeGiT* principle. ('Worship' isn't in this axiom because it is silent!) This "Learn, Grow, Teach™" purpose is what we all have on this earth. It motivates me to stay focused on improving myself, being selfless in my actions and sharing what I have learned with others. And this is where I receive my greatest pleasure.

"He that is greedy of gain troubleth his own house, but he that hateth gifts shall live." Proverbs 15:27

We must remember that none of us is independent unto ourselves; that instead we are dependent on each other for our fulfillment and basic existence. Although we are disconnected physically, we are all connected spiritually. To prosper, I need you as much as I need myself! Paul tells this to us –

"For as we have many members in one body, and all members have not the same office: So we, being many, are one body in Christ, and every one members one of another." Romans 12:4-5

We are all connected and we are all given a spiritual sense. We may deny it or call it something else, but it is real and felt by each of us in some form. In philosophy and psychology, it is called existentialism. In my writings, I refer to is as 'authentic essence."

To verify its existence, think of this: how many times, just as you were thinking of a friend, has the phone rang (or a text pop up) and there he is on the other end! Isn't the first thing you say, "Hey man, I was just thinking of you! I was about to call you!" Again, it is our obligation to tune in to our spiritual sense so we can recognize and respond to it. And more importantly, utilize it properly.

You, my friend, are only an extension of me. And since this is true, how can I afford to treat you ill? It stands to reason that I would only want the best for you, as the best for you is the best for me! We must renew our thinking from independence to codependence and learn the principles so we can teach them to others. By doing this, we all will achieve fulfillment. Indeed, by helping others, we help ourselves.

Benevolence, when practiced, is the most demonstrative form of obedience to the law. It also is the only path prosperity travels. Take the time to identify the path. Then prepare and strengthen yourself for the journey ahead. And know that the walk, trying though it is, is in itself as rewarding as the destination.

✓ Do you find yourself wanting to do more for others? How can you do so?
✓ Are you afraid to give that which you want to give most? If so, why?

I expect to pass through life but once. If, therefore, there be any kindness I can show, or any good thing I can do to any fellow being, let me do it now, for I shall not pass this way again.

William Penn

The Issue of Selfishness

Selfishness. This is not one of the principles but it is so insidious and damaging that it deserves notable mention. *Selfishness* is the characteristic that most severely taints multiple principles simultaneously.

For example - - imagine a person rushing through a tail end of a yellow traffic signal. Let's picture the traffic accident he causes. Through his *selfishness*, we can see that he broke the principles of patience, benevolence, and obedience. He was too impatient to just stop and wait for the next green light. He was too greedy to let someone else go first. He was disobedient to the signal. His *selfishness* caused problems for his fellow man as well as additional problems for himself.

Selfishness is borne out of fear. The fear of being alone, fear of not having, fear of being powerless, the fear of the unknown or the fear of death. *Selfishness* exists only when we lack faith. When we practice faith and love, there is no room for *selfishness* because our desire to obey the law changes our motivations and expectations and creates an uncommon level of insight. When we fill our lives with love and activate the principles, we will achieve the true peace, prosperity and security we desire. We are told,

*"Trust in the LORD, and do good; so shalt thou dwell in the land, and verily thou shalt be fed. Delight thyself also in the LORD; and he shall give thee the **desires** of thine **heart**. Commit thy way unto the LORD; trust also in him; and he shall bring it to pass." Psalms 37:3-5*

We have the choice to obey or disobey. And since God provides us free will, He will allow us to follow through with *our* selfish program. But like the children we are, when the consequences (debt, stress) become overwhelming and unmanageable, we expect Him to just eliminate it and to take away the consequences of our own doing. "Lord, I pray for the elimination of my debt." How selfish is that!?

As a whole, *selfishness* causes a great majority of all human inflictions. All crime is because of greed and *selfishness*. Racism, poverty, war – all start in the spirit of *selfishness*. We can identify injustices such as slavery in America, social inequalities such as poverty in America, and financial harm such as the damage done to investors in the company that fabricated its accounting books as originating in *selfishness*.

If we embrace the principles, *selfishness* ceases to be an issue. Activating the *Biblical Principles to Prosperity* minimizes the environment that breeds *selfishness*.

If you judge people, you have no time to love them.

Mother Theresa

Your Decision, Your Choice, Your Action

We live in a world full of both prosperity and poverty. It can be identified that a person's position in either is a direct reflection of his adherence to Biblical principles.

I pray that throughout this book you have seen that the principles of acknowledging God, faith, obedience, work, creating the unseen, patience and benevolence are all irrevocably codependent and connected. I hope that you have let go of some of the baggage and untruths that you have been carrying and have identified a path to your own prosperity.

As you have read this book, you may feel that you haven't gotten your answers on how to become prosperous. You may feel that the principles are vague and don't explain exactly what to do to become prosperous. Suffice to say that the principles are all that need to be practiced for you to become successful. Or, the principles may come across to you as too simple and shallow. Good; indeed, they are simple. Remember, we are the ones who make our lives difficult by living in the gray area. Jesus said,

"And said, Verily I say unto you, Except ye be converted, and become as little children, ye shall not enter into the kingdom of heaven. Whosoever therefore shall humble himself as this little child, the same is greatest in the kingdom of heaven." Matthew 18:3-4

All this means is that we are to make ourselves as trusting and unbiased and unafraid as children for us to have the faith to do those things that put us in the book of life. Is it simple? Yes. Is it easy? No. But it can be done…by you.

There is one thing I encourage you to do; check out this information! Don't be *"as sheep for the slaughter"* and accept what you read as gospel. That would be an act of a lazy person (and we don't want to disobey the principle of work, do we?) Take the time to research the information. Take the time to reflect on how what you've read compares to your own life, your experiences, your history. Contrast, compare, juxtapose, extrapolate it with your own beliefs and actions. Do you see any differences between what is written in this book and what you know, believe, or do?

I want you to see the principles as truth for yourself. I want you to believe, adopt and practice these principles as your own. Indeed, they are! I want you to be strong and firm in your knowledge and belief so no man can *"...deceive you."*

It is written,

"So faith cometh by hearing, and hearing by the word of God."
Romans 10:17

And Jesus said,

"And every one that heareth these sayings of mine, and doeth them not, shall be likened unto a foolish man, which built his house upon the sand: And the rain descended, and the floods came, and the winds blew, and beat upon that house; and it fell and great was the fall of it."
Matthew 7:26-27

In other words, if you hear this information, research it and have it impressed in your heart but fail to apply it, you will be blown adrift by the winds of life. And honestly, haven't you had enough of that turbulent windstorm in your life? Allow me to reiterate that the law was 'rejected.' And when we reject the law, we cannot complain about the results we receive, as we will have only 'reaped what you sowed.'

Someone out there may be wondering if I have achieved prosperity. I can tell you that in applying the principles in my life, I have achieved prosperity. My prosperity is peace of mind. I am at peace with God, my fellow human beings and myself. But while I endure the trials that this life promises, I can say that I want for nothing. I love and am loved and I eagerly await the return of our Lord so we can all rejoice and praise Him all the daylong!

It is as a true believer that I say that I personally stand by these principles and use them daily in all that I do. In fact, I have gotten to the point where I activate them without thinking about them. It is only after I think about what happened that I connect my actions with the principles. And each time, without fail, I am still amazed! I just give thanks and keep on applying them. Since God is not a *'respecter of persons,'* we know that if I can do it, so can you.

It is with love and full confidence that I urge you to implement the principles in all that you do. And as you do, observe your results. You may receive a blessing here, a blessing there.   You will find your faith building and your confidence stronger. You will also have a new "pep in your step" now that you are in the know.

Here's a kicker - - if you want to really see the principles at work, observe those who do not apply them!   Look at their results!

Remember Joshua 1:8 - -

"This book of the law shall not depart out of thy mouth, but thou shalt meditate therein day and night, that thou mayest observe to do

according to all that is written therein; for then thou shalt make thy way
prosperous, and then thou shalt have good success." Joshua 1:8

If you obey the word of God and apply these *Biblical Principles to Prosperity*, I truly believe that you will be prosperous, as God will have you to be. I pray that you find your path and have a prosperous journey in this walk of life.

I love you as I love myself.

Israel

Learn, Grow, Teach™

Notes

Scriptural Research and Other Readings

References were given for each scripture used throughout the book. I recommend you research them, including the full verse and chapter from which they were taken. Meditate on each of them and allow the Holy Spirit to make them plain to you. I pray that you receive clarity and purpose from the scriptures and adopt the principles within them as your own and incorporate them in your life.

The following four books are just a sample of the many that I have read, studied and meditated on. The information within them guided me to the answers that I was seeking. I highly recommend them as they may be helpful to you and assist you in recognizing your God ordained purpose, plan your path and strengthen you on your walk to prosperity.

- William V. Thompson and Fatin H. Horton, <u>Debt Trap: How Did We Get In? How Do We Get Out?</u>

- Wallace D. Wattles, <u>The Science of Getting Rich</u>

- Florence S. Shinn, <u>The Game of Life and How to Play It</u>

- Napoleon Hill, <u>Think and Grow Rich</u>

Are you activating the Principles?

As the book was being written, characteristics of human frailties came to mind as I was shown each principle. The qualities below each principle are either contrary to the principles or a result of failure to activate the principles. Either way, they prevent true prosperity from being achieved. Notice that a few of the negative qualities show up under more than one principle. This list is not all-inclusive as I am sure you can name more. Take time and reflect on these damaging qualities and how they easily occur and pop up in your daily life. Then strengthen yourself from them.

Acknowledgment

- ✓ Selfishness
- ✓ Foolishness
- ✓ Fear
- ✓ Pride
- ✓

Faith

- ✓ Fear
- ✓ Indecisiveness
- ✓ Impatience
- ✓ Greed
- ✓ Lust
- ✓ Envy
- ✓ Cowardice

Obedience

- ✓ Not applying the principles
- ✓ Not listening to another's wisdom
- ✓ Self-reliance
- ✓ Pride
- ✓ Greed
- ✓

Think It, Write It, Speak It

- ✓ Gossip, Slander
- ✓ Shortsightedness
- ✓ Confusion
- ✓ Restlessness
- ✓ Distraction
- ✓ Complaining, Grumbling
- ✓

Work

- ✓ Laziness
- ✓ Selfishness
- ✓ I 'Deserve' mentality
- ✓ Irresponsibility
- ✓

Patience

- ✓ Debt
- ✓ Anger
- ✓ Frustration
- ✓ Loss
- ✓ Inconsideration
- ✓

Benevolence

- ✓ It's not my job (responsibility)
- ✓ Greed
- ✓ Selfishness
- ✓ Pride
- ✓ Jealousy
- ✓ Inconsideration
- ✓

<u>Seminars, Presentations, Workshops</u>

Let us know what you think! Feel free to offer your testimonies, experiences, as well as your opinions on the book. We believe and fully operate on the principle that we are a team, and each of us is stronger when we work, support and edify each other.

Would you like to learn how to activate the principles directly from the author? Professor Wright is dedicated to informing and educating everyone on the power and effectiveness of the principles and is available to speak at your church, private or public organization. Just contact us with your group name and function, desired speaking date and location, and we will contact you. We truly look forward to meeting, sharing and learning with you.

Visit

<u>www.preceptslifecoaching.com</u>

<u>www.airbornefinancialgroup.com</u>

<u>@airbornefinance</u>

<u>#airbornefinancialgroup</u>